41546

Brassey's *History of Uniforms*

Current titles

Roman Army: Wars of the Empire
Barbarian Warriors: Saxons, Vikings, Normans
American Civil War: Confederate Army
American Civil War: Union Army
Napoleonic Wars: Wellington's Army
Napoleonic Wars: Napoleon's Army
Mexican-American War 1846-48
English Civil War

Forthcoming titles

Spanish-American War 1898
World War One: British Army

Brassey's *History of Uniforms*

Roman Army Wars of the Empire

By Graham Sumner

Colour plates by Graham Turner

Series editor Tim Newark

To my parents

First English Edition 1997

UK editorial offices: Brassey's Ltd, 33 John Street, London WC1N 2AT
UK Orders: Marston Book Services, PO Box 269, Abingdon, OX14 4SD

North American Orders: Brassey's Inc, PO Box 960, Herndon, VA 22070, USA

Graham Sumner has asserted his moral right to be identified as the author of this work.

Library of Congress Cataloging in Publication Data available
British Library Cataloguing in Publication Data
A catalogue record for this book is available from the British Library

ISBN 1 857563 212 0 Hardcover

Typeset by Harold Martin & Redman Ltd.
Originated, printed and bound in Singapore under the supervisison of M.R.M. Graphics Ltd, Winslow, Buckinghamshire.

Contents

Introduction

Prior to 1972, most people would have thought they had a pretty good idea of what a Roman soldier should look like. The classic legionary figure in his strip type armour was a familiar image conjured up from Roman sculpture, in particular Trajan's Column in Rome. Moreover this was an image reinforced by numerous artistic representations over the centuries and the celluloid reconstructions of Hollywood epics. In fact very little attention had been paid by scholars to the armour and equipment of Imperial Rome.

By a strange irony the first modern account which

detailed and attempted to re-construct the Roman body armour known today as *Lorica Segmentata* was published almost simultaneously with the formation of the earliest Roman re-enactment society *The Ermine Street Guard*. H. Russell Robinson, based at the Tower of London armouries, used his extensive knowledge of eastern and oriental armour to re-evaluate the sculptural and archaeological evidence, in particular the important recent discovery of fragments of *Lorica Segmentata* from the site at Corbridge in Northumberland. This ultimately led to the publication of Robinson's book *The Armour of Imperial*

Opposite.
A fine study of a reconstructed Roman legionary.

Reconstructed Roman battle line.

A small metal framed piece of artillery mounted on a cart, shown on Trajan's Column.

Rome in 1974, which in Britain especially was a landmark in the study of Roman Military equipment.

Independently *The Ermine Street Guard*, founded in 1972, had based their initial reconstructions largely on the research of Graham Webster, mostly discounted by Robinson. By chance the two parties met and Robinson, impressed by the Guard members' attitude, freely offered his advice. The resulting stimulus has enabled the Guard, after Robinson's untimely death, to continue to be in the forefront of Roman military research and re-construction.

The past 25 years have seen a wealth of new evidence published, specifically relating to Roman military equipment or the army in general. New theories have been advanced, old ones challenged or even discounted. However most of this material is unavailable to the general reader and the justification of adding this volume to an increasing list is to spread some of this information more widely. An academic reader may therefore find little that is new within these pages, although it is hoped they may discover it proves to be a useful summary of the available evidence and interpretations.

Wherever possible material has been used from periods or regions less familiar than those which normally illustrate publications on the Roman Army. In particular the often overlooked Third Century AD is a fascinating and traumatic era in Roman Imperial history which is proving to be a rich area of study. Other subjects now receiving some long overdue attention are the former Eastern provinces of the Roman Empire. An attempt has therefore been made here to redress this imbalance which has existed between these provinces and those of Britain and Germany where the bulk of the evidence has come from and the majority of scholarly attention focused.

Whereas before, the study of Roman military equipment had attracted very little academic attention, this situation has now been corrected. There have appeared attempts to categorise helmets (Robinson), belt plates (Grew and Griffiths), aprons (Bishop), tunics (Fuentes) and even studies of spear heads (Marchant). One particular and significant change has been the re-assessment of the role of the Roman Cavalry, often seen in the past as an almost ineffective arm of the Imperial army. This change in attitude was a direct result of the research into the Roman saddle by Peter Connolly. The subsequent re-construction of Connolly's saddle and its use by riders such as Ann

Hyland and re-enactors like Marcus Junkelmann, have dramatically demonstrated how effective the cavalry could have been.

After the Civil Wars which brought the republic to an end, Julius Caesar's adopted heir Octavianus was proclaimed 'Augustus' and became in effect the First Emperor. The huge army that Augustus inherited was not entirely loyal, large numbers of troops were disbanded while others were sent to guard the far flung borders of the Empire. For most parts of the early Empire the garrison numbered about thirty legions and perhaps an equal number of Auxiliaries, possibly no more than 500,000 men, a surprisingly small amount when one considers the vast territory that was occupied.

The army that Augustus reformed consisted of the following units. The PRAETORIAN GUARD, the COHORTES URBANAE, the VIGILES, the LEGIONES, COHORTES CIVIUM ROMANORUM, GERMANI CORPORIS CUSTODES, the AUXILIA and the Navy. This book concentrates on the armour and equipment that would have been in use by the Roman soldier on active service. While mention has been made of the equipment termed as 'sports' equipment, this topic is worthy of a publication in its own right, indeed the historian and re-enactor Marcus Junkelmann has only recently published a volume in Germany on this very subject.

The study of the Roman army is not finite and continues apace. New archaeological discoveries add to our overall knowledge but often raises more questions than answers. This publication highlights some of the attempts to answer many of these questions often with controversial results, it is the product of the continual research of academics and re-enactors many known personally by the author and to whom a great debt is owing. Due to this process of ongoing research it is interesting to speculate on the future contents of another corresponding volume published 25 years from now.

A Roman *Centurion*, centre, relaxes with fellow officers in suitably reconstructed accommodation at the Archaeological Park Xanten.

Wars of the Empire

AUGUSTUS 27 BC-AD 14	BC	27	Campaign in Gaul.
		26-25	Campaign against the Cantabri and Astures in Spain.
		16-13	Campaign in Gaul.
		15	Campaign in Raetia by Drusus and TIBERIUS.
		13-9	Campaign in Illyricum.
		12-9	Campaign in Germania by Drusus.
		8-6	Campaign in Germania by TIBERIUS.
	AD	4-6	Campaign in Germania by TIBERIUS.
		6	Revolt in Illyricum and Pannonia.
		9	Defeat of Varus in Germania.
		10-11	Campaign in Germania by TIBERIUS.
TIBERIUS 14 -37 AD		14-16	Campaign in Germania by Germanicus.
		17-24	Revolt in Africa by Tacfarinas.
		21	Revolt in Gaul.
		28	Revolt of the Frisii in Germania.
		34-36	Parthian War.
CLAUDIUS 41 - 54 AD		41-52	Campaign in Mauretania.
			Revolt in Dalmatia.
		43	Invasion of Britannia.
		48	Revolt of the Iceni in Britannia.
		50	Invasion of Germania by Chatii.
		53	Parthians invade Armenia.
NERO 54 - 68 AD		54	Campaign in Spain against Astures.
		58-63	Campaign in Armenia.
		60-61	Revolt of Iceni under Boudica in Britain.
		66-70	Revolt in Judaea, siege of Jerusalem.
		68	Revolt of Vindex in Gaul.
VITELLIUS 69 AD		69	Civil War, final victory by VESPASIANUS.

Opposite.
Reconstructed timber gateway of the first century AD at the
Lunt. Many campaign forts like this had detachments of both
legionaries and Auxiliaries which may explain the variety of
equipment found on these sites.

VESPASIANUS 69-79	69-70	Revolt in Africa.
	71-74	Revolt of Batavians in Germania, siege of Masada. Campaigns in Britannia.
	72	Campaign in Commagene.
	73-74	Campaign in Germania.
	77-78	Campaign against Bructeri.
DOMITIANUS 81 - 96 AD	83	Campaign against Chatti.
	85	Invasion of Moesia by Dacians under Decebalus.
	86-89	Campaign against Dacians.
	89	Revolt of Saturninus, Governor of Germania Superior joined by Chatti.
	92	Campaign against Suebi, Sarmatae and Marcomanii across the Danube.
NERVA 96 - 98 AD	97-98	Campaign against Suebi.
TRAJANUS 98 - 117 AD	101-102	TRAJANUS invades Dacia.
	105-106	Second invasion of Dacia.
	114-117	Invasion of Parthia.
	114	Annexation of Armenia.
	115	Annexation of Mesopotamia.
	115-117	Revolts in Judaea and Egypt.
HADRIANUS 117 - 138	122	Revolt of Moors in Mauretania.
	132-135	Revolt in Judaea.
ANTONINUS PIUS 138 - 161	139	Campaign in Britannia.
	152	Campaign against the Moors in Mauretania.
	157-158	Campaign in Dacia.
MARCUS AURELIUS 161 - 180 AD	162-166	Campaign against the Parthians.
	166-175	Campaigns against Marcomanni, Quadi and Sarmatae in Germania.
	171-172	Revolt in Egypt.
	177	Campaign in Mauretania.
	178-180	Campaigns in Germania.
COMMODUS 180 - 192 AD	180-184	Campaign in Britannia.
	188-	Revolt in Germania.
	193-197	Civil War, final victory by SEPTIMIUS SEVERUS.
SEPTIMIUS SEVERUS 193-211 AD	197-199	Campaigns in Parthia.
	208-211	Campaign in Britannia.
CARACALLA 211-217 AD	213	Campaign in Germania against Alamanni.
MACRINUS 217 - 218 AD	217	Persians defeat MACRINUS.
ELAGABALUS 218 - 222 AD	218	ELAGABULUS defeats MACRINUS.

ALEXANDER SEVERUS 222 - 235 AD	230	Persians invade Mesopotamia.
	232	Campaign against Persians.
	234	Campaign against Alamanni.
MAXIMINUS I 235 - 238 AD	235	Campaign against Alamanni.
	236	Campaign against Dacians and Sarmatae.
	237	Persians invade Mesopotamia.
GORDIANUS III 238 - 244 AD	240	Invasion of Moesia by Goths and Carpi.
	242	Campaign against Persians.
PHILIPPUS I 244-249 AD	245-247	Campaign against Carpi and Quadi.
	247	Invasion of Moesia by Goths and Carpi.
	248	Campaign in Moesia by DECIUS.
TRAJANUS DECIUS 249 - 251 AD	249	Invasion of Dacian provinces by Goths and Carpi.
	251	Defeat and death of DECIUS by Goths.
TREBONIANUS GALLUS 251 - 253 AD	252	Goths invade Northern frontier and Asia minor, Persians invade Mesopotamia.
AEMILIANUS 253 AD	253	Campaign against Goths in Moesia.
VALERIANUS 253 - 260	254	Marcomanni invade Pannonia. Invasion of Thrace by Goths. Persians invade Mesopotamia.
	256	Goths attack Asia Minor. Franks invade Germania inferior.
	258	Campaign against Goths by GALLIENUS.
	260	VALERIANUS defeated and captured by Persians.
GALLIENUS 253 - 268	260	Postumus declares separate Empire in Gaul. Revolts in Pannonia, Persians invade Syria Asia and Cappadocia Persians defeated by Macrianus.
	262-267	Campaigns against Persians by Odenathus of Palmyra.
	263	Unsuccessful campaign against Postumus.
	267	Goths invade Thrace and Greece.
	268	Goths invade Asia Minor but defeated by GALLIENUS.
CLAUDIUS II (GOTHICUS) 270 - 275	268	Invasion of Raetia and Italia by Alamanni defeated by CLAUDIUS II.
	269	CLAUDIUS II defeats Goths.
AURELIANUS 270 - 275	270	Dacia abandoned. Palmyrenes led by Zenobia invade Egypt. AURELIANUS defeats German tribes in Italy and the Vandals in Pannonia, invasion of Italy by Alamanni and Marcomanni defeated. AURELIANUS campaigns against Zenobia, revolt in Egypt crushed. Palmyra sacked.
	271-273	AURELIANUS defeats separatist Empire in Gaul. Invasion of Raetia repelled.
	274	AURELIANUS hailed as RESTITVTOR PACATOR ORBIS 'restorer and pacifier of the world'.

14 Army Organisation

Army Organisation

The Praetorian Guard

The Imperial bodyguard was a hand picked elite infantry unit which varied in size according to the dictates of succeeding Emperors. Its initial formation under Augustus was nine Cohorts of 500 men each, this was increased by Caligula to twelve, later sixteen by Vitellius during the Civil War of AD 69. Vespasianus reduced this number again to nine, but the number was soon raised once more, this time to ten by Domitianus the son of Vespasianus. Each Cohort was commanded by a Tribune and two Roman knights (equestrians) took overall command as Praetorian Prefects. The Cohorts were probably divided on legionary lines into Centuries of 80 men. After about five years service infantrymen could be promoted to cavalrymen (*equites*) attached to the Centuries. There was originally a small elite cavalry force, the SPECULATORES AUGUSTI, but by the Second Century there was additionally the Imperial Horse Guards EQUITES SINQULARES AUGUSTI. These were men seconded from amongst the best of the frontier Auxiliary cavalry units and were probably organised like a regular Cavalry ALA with about 450 men.

The early Emperors attempted to play down their reliance on the military for political support, so the guard are often referred to as wearing civilian clothes, but this could mean an off duty tunic and side arms. Both infantry and cavalrymen probably wore similar equipment to regular Legions and ALA but obviously reflecting their higher status and pay. Another possibility is that like soldiers today many of their ceremonial equipment would be of a traditional

Opposite.
Early Imperial Centurion. This reconstruction wears a mail shirt with shoulder doubling and chest fastener. He wears his sword on the left side unlike the legionaries and plain bronze silvered greaves. The transverse horse hair crest would help to further distinguish this soldier in battle.

nature. Modern authorities suggest scale armour was widely used by Praetorians, while the Scorpion emblem, the birth sign of the Emperor Tiberius, is often associated with Guard shields and standards.

Most of the early Emperors also seem to have had some form of horse guard but by the early Second century A.D. an Imperial Horse Guard, EQUITES SINGULARES AUGUSTI had formally been created either by Domitianus or Trajanus. Following the fashion of the Provincial Governors who selected a bodyguard from amongst the Auxiliary troops under their command, the men of the Horse Guard were hand picked from amongst the elite cavalry units of the Empire. One suggestion is that when Trajanus, previously a provincial Governor, was proclaimed Emperor he simply promoted his own provincial bodyguard to an Imperial bodyguard, as at least he could rely on their loyalty.

The EQUITES SINGULARES AUGUSTI were based in their own camp in Rome and were probably organised as a normal cavalry unit. After selection troopers served in the horse guard until their retirement. It is not certain if the troopers wore any official uniform or carried any particular insignia. If they retained their own provincial equipment which they may have personally bought, this might have highlighted their unique character. A similar situation was created by officers in the First World War who after joining the newly formed Royal Flying Corps proudly kept their original regimental uniforms and cap badges.

The Urban Cohorts (*Cohortes Urbanae*)

Towards the end of his reign Augustus appears to have raised the Praetorian Guard strength to twelve Cohorts, but the three newly raised Cohorts were apparently re-designated as COHORTES URBANAE. Their main duties according to the historian Tacitus were to act as a City police force. Further Cohorts were created but were sent to other cities such as Ostia, the Port of Rome, or even outside Italy to Carthage and Lyon . The Cohorts sent to this latter city were responsible for guarding an Imperial mint, established there by Augustus.

The Vigiles

Created by Augustus in AD 6, the main task of the VIGILES was to combat fires which were always a serious risk in Rome. Severn Cohorts were established with a strength of 1000 men each. The force was commanded by an equestrian *Praefectus* with a *Tribunus* in command of each Cohort.

The VIGILES were equipped with portable fire engines complete with pump operated hoses. In addition to this, there were small *Ballistae* used for

projecting hooks or stone missiles to demolish buildings. While clearly operating on military lines and regarded as part of the army establishment, offered excellent prospects for promotion, but it is unlikely the VIGILES wore legionary type armour other than a helmet. An early bronze *Italic* helmet from Herculaneum is said to have belonged to a member of the VIGILES based in that town.

The German Bodyguard (GERMANI CORPORIS CUSTODES)

The GERMANI CORPORIS CUSTODES bodyguard was a personal bodyguard of the early Emperors in addition to the PRAETORIAN GUARD. They were recruited almost entirely from two German tribes, the Batavii and Ubii, and were considered far more reliable than the easily corruptible Italians serving in the PRAETORIAN GUARD! As they were basically the Emperors private army a considerable amount of money may have been lavished

First Century reliefs of *Praetorians*. The figure on the left is from a famous sculpture now in the Louvre which has been highly influential in the early perception of the PRAETORIAN GUARD. The second figure is from the Cancellaria relief in Rome. The shield carried by this figure is seen as evidence for the PRAETORIAN GUARD using slightly archaic equipment. The method of holding the Pila has generally been adopted by re-enactors. All the *Pila* on this sculpture have an additional weight for extra penetration. Figures on the Cancellaria relief have also provided details of open toed and heeled socks worn beneath the sandals.

M. Aurelius Lucianus served with the PRAETORIAN GUARD. His tombstone shows him in undress tunic but reveals other fascinating details including the double weighted Pila with bound shaft, and elaborate eagle headed pommel just visible behind the broad decorated baldric, in his right hand he wields a *Fustis*.

The Roman Historian Cassius Dio records that the Praetorians in his day, that is the early Third Century AD, wore scale armour. This figure on the Column of Marcus Aurelius may therefore represent one member of the Guard and it is believed scale is used as a device to distinguish Guard members on this monument.

on their armour and equipment. The bodyguard operated as both cavalry and infantry and appear to have reached a strength of about 300 men commanded by the Emperor himself.

The German bodyguard was disbanded in AD 69 by Galba and many members of the guard may have joined in the revolt of their kinsman Julius Civilis, forming his own bodyguard until the revolt was put down two years later.

The Legions (LEGIONES)

The Legions were the backbone of the Imperial army, superbly armoured, equipped and trained heavy infantry. They were recruited entirely of Roman Citizens, which as citizenship spread amongst the provinces meant that less and less men of Italian origin joined the legions.

Up until the reign of Vespasianus, an Imperial Legion comprised ten Cohorts sub divided into six

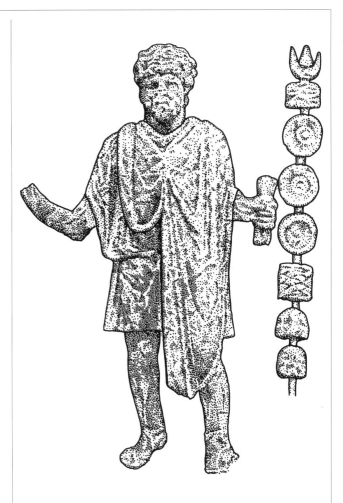

Standard Bearer of the EQUITES SINGULARES AUGUSTI.

Centuries of eighty men making a fighting strength of 4,800. The first Cohort was later made up of five double centuries raising this number to 5,120 men. In all there were about thirty Imperial Legions in the First Century AD. Literary sources often put a Legion at a strength of 6,000 men, which may therefore include a number of non-combatants. In addition to the infantry a small force of 120 cavalrymen was divided amongst the Centuries. They acted as scouts and dispatch riders.

The Legion was commanded by a specially appointed representative of the Emperor, the *Legatus Legionis* (Legate) a member of the Senatorial Class. A Legate was assisted by six military tribunes, five from the Equestrian Class and a senior *Tribunus Laticlavius*, like the Legate, also from the Senatorial Class. Both the Legate and Senior Tribune were entitled to wear a broad purple stripe on their tunics while those from the equestrian order had a narrower one. Other distinguishing features of officers' uniforms were a narrow linen sash tied around the waist and a small dagger called a *Parazonium*. All of these officers were not career soldiers who served for life but as a step in their political careers, without exception they would

Another reconstructed Centurion, this time of the middle First Century AD. Based on the Tombstone of M. Favonius Facilis in Colchester.

be fairly young men. The most famous Governor of Roman Britain, Gn. Julius Agricola, was only 28 when he was a Legate commanding LEGIO XX based in Northern Britain. Therefore the officer with most experience within a Legion was technically the Third in Command, the *Praefectus Castrorum* (Camp Prefect). He had formally been a *Primus Pilus* 'Centurion Chief' who had literally spent all his adult life in the army.

The Centurions are often equated with the modern rank of Sergeant Major, conjuring up the image of a tough Marine sergeant drilling raw recruits. However as the 60 Centurions were of graded seniority, they had a much wider range of responsibilities. The *Primus Pilus* was commander of the First Century in the First Cohort. Next in line was the *Princeps*, followed by the *Hastatus*, *Princeps Posterior* and *Hastatus Posterior*. Centurions in all the other Cohorts were ranked as *Pilus Prior*, *Pilus Posterior*, *Princeps Prior*, *Hastatus Prior* and *Hastatus Posterior*. The distinguishing emblems of the Centurion were his Transverse Crest, of either feathers or horsehair, a cloak worn over the left shoulder and his vine stick. In the first Century AD, Centurions are the only soldiers who officially wore Greaves on their legs.

Beneath the Centurion was his deputy the *Optiones* (Optio) chosen by him from amongst the men in his Century. *Optiones* designated as Centurions elect but waiting for a vacancy were termed *Optiones Ad Spem Ordinis*. Other ranks in the Century were the *Signifer* (Standard bearer) and an officer in charge of the watch *Tesserarius*. Various other soldiers could serve on to the headquarters staff *Tabularium Legionis* as accountants and clerks or police officers. Soldiers picked out of the ranks for special duties, *Beneficiarii*, could serve on the staff of the Provincial Governors.

A whole range of other posts were available to ordinary soldiers and their duties would literally make them *Immunes*, immune from the more unpleasant tasks. *Immunes* acted as doctors, medics, hospital orderlies, carpenters, engineers, blacksmiths, hunters, clerks, stonemasons, architects, armourers, grooms and even priests. This pool of talent was often made available for civil as well as military building projects.

Recruitment was generally voluntary and recruits had to pass a medical examination and be at least six Roman feet in height. If recruits could pass the examination, age did not matter and the youngest known recruit was 13! Proof was required of citizenship and references were essential. Officially the Roman army was not the last refuge for drop outs or 'the scum of the earth'. From the reign of Vespasianus, service was for 25 years and on retirement the soldier was given a cash donation or, until the time of Hadrianus, an allotment of land, probably in a Colony. Veterans too were largely exempt from taxation.

Citizen Cohorts (COHORTES CIVIUM ROMANORUM VOLUNTARIORUM/ INGENUORUM)

In times of emergency Augustus recruited Cohorts of Citizens, thirty two were raised during the Pannonian revolt and six Cohorts were enrolled in the wake of the Varian disaster in AD9. The urgency with which they were raised and trained suggests the standard of recruits and level of training in the Cohorts was not as rigorous as that enforced in the Legions. Citizen Cohorts that were retained on the establishment eventually recruited non Roman Citizens as well. As Citizens, it should be expected that the average soldier was better equipped than his Auxiliary counterpart but this is far from certain.

The Auxilia

One of the major reforms of Augustus was the

reorganisation of the Auxiliary forces into regular units, although this may just have recognised a situation that was already happening. Auxiliaries were recruited because they could provide specialist skills lacking in the legions, most importantly mounted units.

By the Second century AD, there were six types of Auxiliary unit: Infantry *COHORS*, Cavalry *ALA* and mixed units of Cavalry and Infantry, the *COHORTES EQUITATAE*. These came in five hundred and one thousand strong units, the elite was the one thousand strong *Ala Miliaria* of which only one unit was stationed in any one particular province. In Britain for example the ALA AUGUSTA GALLORUM PETRIANA MILLIARIA CIVIUM ROMANORUM BIS TORQUATA was based at Stanwix on Hadrian's Wall. The official numerical designation provided a paper strength only and surviving rosters show units well below these figures.

Auxiliaries were granted Roman citizenship on completion of 25 years service and presented with a

An early Imperial *Optio*, second in command to a Centurion, a reconstruction based on the equipment worn by Gaius Valerius Crispus, a legionary from Wiesbaden. Apart from the knobbed staff and a finger ring there are no other known features that would distinguish an *Optio* from other legionaries.

diploma as proof of this, as an important incentive for recruitment. More cynical commentators might see the high pay that Auxiliaries received as a more likely inducement. Recent research has shown basic infantry pay was nearly five sixths that of a legionary's and not one third as previously believed. A cavalryman received the same pay as a legionary. This helps explain the equally lavish auxiliary tombstones and transfers between Auxiliary and legionary units.

Auxiliary infantry units were organised along legionary lines that is the cohorts were sub-divided into Centuries commanded by Centurions. Most of the other legionary junior ranks would also be found but until the Second century Auxiliaries would not have participated in the major construction activities, so the number of *Immunes* that may have existed in Auxiliary units would have been considerably less. Cavalry units were sub-divided into TURMAE of about thirty men commanded by the cavalry equivalent of the Centurion called a *Decurion*. The organisation of the COHORTES EQUITATAE units is more problematical and historians are not quite sure whether the infantry centurions had either sixty or eighty men, like the regular infantry Cohorts. While there was only one known ALA of camel mounted

Reconstructed *Optio* from the Flavian period c. 69-96 AD.

An *Optio* on a Grave Stelae from Apamea.

Third Century *Decurion* from the **EQUITIES SINGULARES AUGUSTI** on a Grave Stela from Rome.

troops, ALA I ULPIA DROMEDARIORUM, many units stationed in the cast seem to have had a small detachment of camel riders as well.

Prefects commanded the infantry COHORS and cavalry ALA although sometimes the larger units were led by *Tribunes*. In both cases the officers were from the Equestrian class. The career structure established in the Roman army meant that some of these officers were ex-centurions from the Legions. Just as the British Army in the Nineteenth century had initial difficulties with sending Indian troops abroad so the Romans did too, indeed the Thracians revolted during the reign of Tiberius after hearing rumours they were to be sent to another part of the Empire. Almost certainly the practice of maintaining units in or near their homeland was abandoned after the Batavian revolt which eventually required eight legions to suppress!

In the First century AD, Auxiliaries were normally recruited from amongst the free peoples of the frontier provinces, either by voluntary means, tribal levies or forced conscription. Units were given ethnic titles and for a while the recruits would be from the region of origin. As the century wore on this system began to break down. As units were settled in frontier provinces after a period of years, local recruitment would gradually delete the original composition of the unit. In addition Roman Citizens found service in the Auxilia increasingly attractive, either because they were ineligible in some way for service in the legions or they found the pay and conditions suitable. Provincial Governors selected their bodyguard from the Auxilia stationed with in their own province. The body guard *SINGULARES* was probably the equivalent in size to a mixed Cohort.

In 212 AD, the Emperor Caracalla granted citizenship to all free born inhabitants of the Empire. This immediately made the differences between legionary and Auxiliary service obsolete, although it would only have been a matter of time before the process begun by Augustus would have reached this inevitable conclusion.

Numeri and Cunei

The original thinking behind the Auxilia had been to introduce a flexible element and new fighting skills into the army. As the Auxilia became more regular and

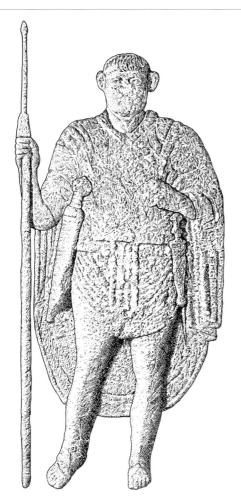

C. Petilius Secundus, a legionary with **LEGIO XV PRIMIGENIA** on a tombstone from Bonn. The weight on the *Pila* can clearly be seen as well as the normal arrangement of sword and dagger.

Statius Rufus, a seaman with the Imperial fleet based at Misenum, shown on his tombstone from Athens, Second Century AD.

adopted standard equipment, the need once more arose to recreate irregular units. One answer effected was the creation of the NUMERI and CUNEI from amongst peoples on both sides of the Imperial frontier. NUMERI originally used their own weapons and were probably commanded by their own native chieftains. This situation was reflected in the individual unit titles such as the NUMERUS HNAUDIFRIDI named after a commander called Hnaudifridus or Notfried, or the NUMERUS MILITUM SYRORUM SAGITTARIORUM, a unit of Syrian archers. Other units were named after a particular function which they carried out, such as the VENATORES BANNIENSES, the hunters from

Banna, or the NUMERUS BARCARIORUM TIGRISENSIUM, a unit of bargemen from the river Tigris.

Cavalry units were often referred to as CUNEUS or wedge but are also called NUMERUS on occasion, perhaps indicative of their flexible nature. The majority of these irregular units would not have been as well paid as the regular Auxiliaries and they did not receive Citizenship after discharge from the army.

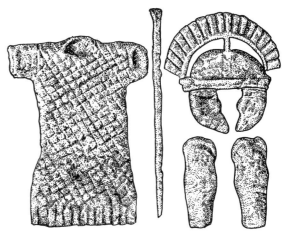

Armour and equipment of the *Centurio* T. Caldius Severus shown on his tombstone at Carnuntum. This sculpture and one of a helmet belonging to Marcus Petronius Classicus from Ptuj, plus a description from the late Roman historian Vegetius are the only pieces of evidence for the wearing of Transverse Crests by Centurions.

Early Augustan legionary infantryman. This reconstruction like all others of this period is influenced by the Alter of Domitius Ahenobarbus from Rome showing Republican figures in some detail. He wears a Montefortino helmet with a black horse hair crest, a mail shirt with shoulder doubling and a 'Mainz' type sword. The large shield is based on the example found in the Fayum region of Egypt.

Therefore this lower grade status was inevitably reflected in their equipment. Native style clothing and weapons such as the *Gaesum*, a socketed spear with a slender neck and barbed head or even the Dacian *falx* were probably used initially but replacement weapons might have been made by blacksmiths based in the frontier forts, so over time more standardised equipment may have been gradually introduced. A few specialised units of NUMERI may have had pay and service conditions on a par with the Auxilia and may even have attracted Citizens into their ranks. The most famous of these specialist units are the scouts, EXPLORATORES, attached to the frontier forts.

These units if they had been stationed at a particular site for a number of years included the place name in their title. An example of this is the NUMERUS EXPLORATORUM HABITANCENSIUM named after Habitancum, modern day Risingham, NUMERI manned outposts forts or signal towers and reinforced existing Auxiliary units relieving some of the burden of policing and patrol duties.

The Navy

The Roman Navy is the poor relation in the study of the Roman Military. However the Navy did have an important role to play in protecting the sea ways and major rivers, controlling piracy and transporting troops and supplies.Augustus would also not have forgotten that it was his naval victory over the forces of Antony and Cleopatra at Actium in 27 BC that had brought him to power. The two main Naval bases established by Augustus were at Ravenna and Misenum, with detachments later dotted around the Mediterranean and along the Rhine and Danube.

Fleet commanders were *Praefecti* from the equestrian order with similar status to Auxiliary commanders. Beneath this rank the system is not so clear, as the Romans were never ones to fully appreciate Naval intricacies, largely adopting Greek principles. Naval Squadron Commanders appear to

Detail of a reconstructed staff and ring belonging to an *Optio*. Both of these were badges of office. The ring is based on an example from Bonn.

have had the title *Navarch*, while individual ship's captains were called *Trierarchs*. A ship also had a *Centurio* complete with administrative staff, an *Optio* and a detachment of infantry. One can imagine sometimes the friction between *Trierarchs* and *Centurions* as a result of their dual command.

Service in the fleet was for twenty-six years and on discharge the sailors were granted Citizenship. Occasionally in emergencies the navy even provided a source of recruits for the legions. Both LEGIO I and LEGIO II ADIUTRIX were formed this way and Hadrian reinforced LEGIO X FRETENSIS with a draft of sailors. Another activity of the navy appears to have been the manning of the rigging involved in the awnings for the great amphitheatres.

We can only guess what effect the long periods of inactivity must have had on the morale of the navy. For over two hundred years after the death of Augustus the Romans faced no serious naval challenge. When it did come in the Third century in the form of increased raids in the West and East the navy like other branches of the army was often unable to cope effectively.

Standard Bearers and Musicians

Roman standards were sacred, revered objects. When not in use in the field they were kept in a shrine within the fortress or fort. On special occasions garlands or laurel wreaths were placed on them and they were anointed with oils. Loss of the Eagle standards in battle would be a disgrace and units that did so were often disbanded. Augustus instigated a campaign to recover the Eagles lost in the defeat of Varus in AD 9, while the recovery of Eagle standards from the Parthians was hailed as a diplomatic triumph.

The standards had a practical function as well as a religious one. Standards were placed in the ground to mark out the site of the camp at the end of a day's march and woe betide a commander if the standard bearers were unable to move them the next day. In the chaos and confusion of battle the standards would be used to relay orders. Attention was drawn to them by blasts on the horns by the musicians who were always in close attendance. Very basic orders such as move backwards or forwards could be easily conveyed by a simple movement.

The most famous standard used by the Romans was the Eagle standard *Aquila*, a single one for each legion carried by an *Aquilifer*. Republican Eagles were

Reconstructed Auxiliary troops advance in open order. The advantage of these units was their flexibility combining skirmishing tactics with the ability to fight in more rigid formations.

Opposite.

Top left.

Marching Legionary from the Adamklissi Tropaeum. None of the troops on this monument are equipped with the elaborate marching pack depicted on the near contemporary Trajan's Column.

Top right.

A legionary soldier from the Adamklissi Tropaeum, of interest is the fact that he is wearing his sword on his left side.

Bottom left.

Two legionaries on a column base from Mainz dating to the time of Vespasianus. The background legionary brings up his shield into the face of an unseen enemy. Surprisingly there is no indication of the *Lorica Segmentata* or other form of body armour unless it is worn under a fabric covering.

Bottom right.

Standard Bearer from Budapest, Third century AD.

Aurelius Moucianos, a legionary with LEGIO II PARTHICA based at Apamea in the early Third Century, he wears off duty long sleeved tunic and cloak and a ring buckle belt from which two straps with terminals can be seen hanging on his right . Just showing beneath the oval shield can be seen a long *Spatha* sword with a circular chape.

made entirely of silver but by 45 BC they had received gold thunderbolts. Later while the Praetorian Eagle may have been solid gold those in ordinary legions were very likely gilded silver.

Each Century had its own standard *Signum* carried by a *Signifer*, on Trajan's Column standards topped with an outstretched hand *Manus* are shown. This has frequently been taken to refer to a *Maniple* an old republican formation made up of two Centuries, the memory of which may have been preserved by Centurial standards. Another feature of standards depicted on sculptures are a number of discs fixed to the staff. The exact significance of these is not clear and it is sometimes suggested they may indicate the number of the Cohort to which the Century belonged.

Other types of standard included deities, or emblems from the Zodiac which usually represented an Emperor's birth sign. One particularly important standard was the '*Imago*' or image of the ruling Emperor carried by the *Imaginifer*, the only way many of the troops would actually see their commander in

Verinius Marinus *Librarivs* on the headquarters staff of LEGIO II PARTHICA who died at Apamea C 217-220 AD. Long sleeved tunics were universal by this date and ring buckles were fairly common. Marinus holds a scroll in his right hand and a document case in his left.

Reconstructed Auxiliary infantryman, middle First century AD. The helmet is based on a well preserved bronze example found at Mainz. The double belts, sword, and dagger are based on both archaeological finds and the sculptural evidence from First century Grave Stelae. Most re-enactors depicting this period use 'Trajan Column' as the source for shield designs.

Early First century AD cavalryman. This reconstruction is based on contemporary Gallic reliefs and the Arch of Orange. At that date there does not appear to have been a standard cavalry helmet so this figure wears a Coolus type. Unlike cavalrymen on later reliefs those on the Arch of Orange clearly wear no breeches. The oval shield is slightly elongated providing better protection than those used by infantrymen.

chief. Carried by a *Vexilliarius*, the *Vexillium* was a flag type standard which was used to denote which Legio or unit a detachment separated from the main body had come from. These detachments used for building projects or battle groups are known as *Vexillations* after the banner they carried. The *Vexillium* would therefore depict in some manner the unit number and emblem, but what may be an actual *Vexillium* found in Egypt bears instead an image of the Goddess Victory standing on a globe. This could suggest units may also have used other types of flag standard, with the exception of the Eagle, all other types of standard would also be applicable to the Auxilia.

In common with the Celts and other ancient peoples, Roman standard bearers wore animal skins over their helmets. Judging from the evidence available, Praetorian standard bearers used skins from the exotic big cats, like lions and tigers. Legionary and

Auxiliary standard bearers wore either bear or wolf skins, although it may appear for some reason the face of the animal was not worn by standard bearers in the Auxilia. It would have been impractical for Cavalrymen to wear an animal skin so it is not surprising that cavalry standard bearers don't seem to have worn any.

On Trajan's Column the musicians wear animal skins and always appear close to the standard bearers. The most spectacular instrument used by the army was the large circular *Cornu* carried by a *Cornicen*. The

Opposite.
Detail of a reconstructed *Signum* standard showing the silvered bronze discs, pendants and hand *manus* emblem. In keeping with other standard bearers and musicians this standard bearer wears an animal skin, in this case a brown bear, over his helmet.

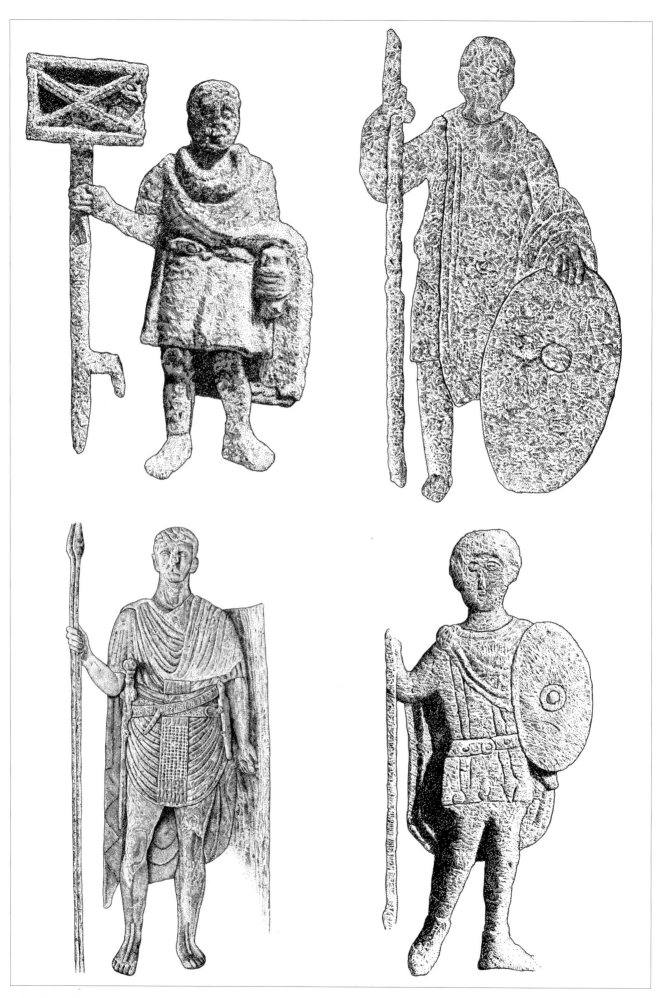

Opposite.
Top left.
Aquilifer from Apamea, Third century AD.

Top right.
This Grave Stela from Amiens shows Valerius Ianuarius, an *Imaginifer* with the **NUMERUS URSARIENSIUM.**

Bottom left.
One of the best preserved First century AD tombstones is that of Annaius Daverzus, an Auxiliary soldier in **COHORS IIII DELMATARUM** a unit recruited from the Balkans and later stationed at Hardknott Fort in Cumbria. Annaius has two floral design belts and while the dagger frog is clearly shown the sword appears to be suspended by another method. Two spears are carried and a flat rectangular shield. The tunic is elaborately folded suggestive of very fine material.

Bottom right.
Compared with the tombstone of Annaius, that of his unknown colleague in **COHORS IIII MILLIARIA TUNGRORUM from Rabat** is executed in a naïve provincial style.

An Auxiliary soldier on the column of Marcus Aurelius.

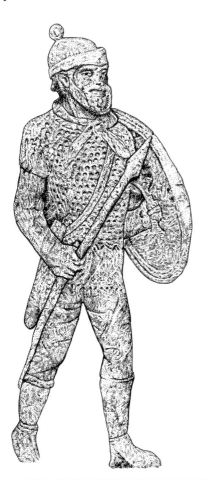

Cornu was also used at religious ceremonies or addresses by the commander. The origins of the *Cornu* were almost certainly Etruscan and probably most other instruments used by the Romans were as well. *Cornus* were used in Civil processions and Gladiatorial displays perhaps even played by military personnel and it may have been in this context that a *Cornu* was left in a repair shop in Pompeii. Another instrument used to draw attention to the standards was the *Tuba* played by a *Tubicen*. The *Tuba* was a long straight instrument about a metre long used to sound the advance and retreat. Both *Cornu* and *Tuba* would have had to have been audible above the sound of battle.

Two other instruments were certainly used by the military, the *Bucina* played by a *Bucinator* and a *lituus*. Little is known of the *Bucina*, on one tombstone it appears like a trombone but this might be a sculptural distortion to fit it in to the confined space on the monument. The *Lituus* was a 'J' shaped instrument and a completely preserved example was found at the Saalburg fort. It has been suggested that the *Lituus* may have been used by the cavalry.

Sibbaeus, an Auxiliary Tubicen with **COHORS I ITURAEORUM** from Mainz. The *Tuba* was about 1.40m long but came in two or three sections which is how it appears to be represented here.

One of the most famous of military formations from the Roman period is the *Testudo* or tortoise, here demonstrated by members of the *Ermine Street Guard*. Impervious to most missiles it was of course not proof against boiling oil or water. The defenders of Cremona hurled one of their own artillery machines down on to a *Testudo* crushing it but pulling down part of the wall as well.

Trajan's Column depicts both standard bearers and some musicians carrying a small round shield. Two leather covers for small circular shields were found at Castleford and these could well have belonged to standard bearers or musicians.

Right.
Highly decorated Centurion from the time of Vespasianus, this reconstruction includes decorated greaves based on those of Q. Sertorius Festus from LEGIO XI CLAUDIA PIA FIDELIS on his tombstone from Verona. The awards include a set of seven Phalerae on a leather harness, two torques worn on a strap around the neck and a pair of *armilla* on each wrist.

Opposite.
Cavalry equipment of the First century AD. Based mainly on the tombstone now in Mainz of C. Romanius Capito who served in the ALAE NORICORVM.

Reconstructing Roman Armour

Roman art and architecture and the achievements of the first professional army continue to have a deep and profound effect on the Western tradition. No other army in European history, arguably the world, endured as long or occupied so vast a territory as the Roman army. While it may be popular today to denigrate the methods and motives of Imperialism, the Roman army will always be remembered and respected.

Numerous sculptures and portraits from the Roman era survive throughout Europe and North Africa, and one historian recently remarked that more British people today would recognise a picture of a Roman Emperor before that of many former Prime Ministers. Not surprisingly, the military traditions, tactics and weaponry from the height of Rome's greatness have been a source of inspiration for generations of Imperial successors from Charlemagne to Hitler. Roman style helmets, swords, breastplates and all the trappings of Imperial insignia have found their way into armies ever since.

Throughout the Middle Ages, artists were faced with the problem of depicting Roman soldiers in religious scenes such as The Crucifixion or Resurrection. Many simply choose to represent them in contemporary arms and armour providing information for the student of medieval armour rather than the Roman. However, one Renaissance artist Andrea Mantegna (1431-1506 A.D) from Padua clearly recognised that the events of Christ's life had taken place during the Roman era. Therefore he tried to accurately represent the Roman soldiers within his paintings wearing the type of armour and equipment visible on the monuments that were at that time being re-discovered. This attention to historic detail is evident when one sees many of Mantegna's works, *The Triumph of Caesar* for example, or the series of paintings depicting the trial and execution of St James in the Eremitani Chapel, sadly destroyed by bombing in the Second World War and known today only by photographs.

By the Nineteenth century, subjects which dealt specifically with Roman as opposed to religious themes appeared. Very often those works reflected Victorian morals and attitudes or affiliations with ancient Roman virtues and Imperialism. By and large artists continued to use sculpture as their main source of evidence, until the new science of archaeology came into being in the latter half of the century. Influenced by the growing collections in museums or even by their own studies at ruins like Pompeii and Herculaneum, artists like Alma-Tadema now included actual archaeological artefacts in their paintings. This of course included military equipment. This approach is obvious when one views a painting by Alma-Tadema entitled *A Silent Greeting* finished in 1889, featuring a Roman officer courting a young lady. Alma-Tadema added a sword scabbard which is a faithful copy of the so called 'Sword of Tiberius' displayed in the British Museum. In addition the soldier's leather cuirass was influenced by that apparently worn on the Tombstone of Valerius Crispus from Wiesbaden.

Alma-Tadema was always highly regarded by the Victorian establishment for the accuracy of his ancient Roman scenes. Apart from a couple of notable exceptions including the future Emperor Titus in full armour or members of the Praetorian Guard at the accession of Claudius, it is a pity that Alma-Tadema did not paint more military figures as this would have shed a lot of light on how Roman armour was perceived in the Nineteenth century. Nevertheless one example by another equally skilled artist does exist from this period, perhaps the most important re-construction until the work of Russell Robinson in the 1960s.

Edward John Poynter's masterpiece *Faithful unto death*, exhibited at the Royal Academy in 1865, represents a Roman soldier standing stoically at his post while in the background Pompeii is destroyed by the eruption of Vesuvius. The circumstances behind

By the end of the Nineteenth century artists like Edward John Poynter were inspired by the latest evidence from archaeological excavations. Poynter himself claimed this painting *Faithful unto death* was based on the remains of a Roman soldier found at Pompeii. © Walker Art Gallery, Liverpool.

Reconstruction of the Heddernheim cavalry helmet produced for the film *Fall of the Roman Empire.* © DCM 65.

this painting are quite remarkable because Poynter announced that he had based his scene on the discovery of the body of a Roman soldier in full armour near to the Herculaneum gate at Pompeii. This is a discovery long since forgotten, but a similar fate also seems to have befallen the so called soldier recently excavated from Herculaneum itself.

Poynter's picture can be viewed as representing obedience to duty and Imperial authority, both popular sentiments in Victorian times.

Faithful unto death was highly successful, encouraging Poynter to paint another critically acclaimed work entitled *The Catapult* in 1868. Not surprisingly, a catapult is the centrepiece of an event during the Roman siege of Carthage. The catapult itself, ostensibly a type of artillery piece referred to today as an *Onager* was acclaimed in its day for its authentic archaeological detail. Both of Poynter's paintings appeared for many years in Victorian and Edwardian history books illustrating aspects of Roman

life long after the appeal of artists such as Poynter and Alma-Tadema had diminished.

These paintings also remained influential in another completely unexpected phenomenon, the Cinema. A study of early Hollywood epics reveals that directors like Cecil B de Mille were familiar with the works of Victorian artists especially Alma-Tadema. Alma-Tadema had also been commissioned to design sets and costumes for theatrical productions paying the same attention to those projects as he did to his paintings and these proved to be another source of inspiration. If the reader is not convinced, look at Alma-Tadema's *Anthony and Cleopatra* before viewing the silent version of *Ben-Hur.*

Soon more scientific approaches were being made in the field of armour and equipment. Following on from excavations at Carnuntum in Austria. The eminent scholar Dr Von Groller attempted to unravel the fragmentary remains of Roman armour discovered in a building identified as an armoury. Von Groller tried to reconcile these fragments with Trajan's Column and believed the metal strips of the *Lorica Segmentata* had to be attached to a less rigid

Second Battle of Cremona, 69 AD

The painting opposite shows a tragic episode from this Civil War battle as described by Vipstanus Messalla. A recent recruit serving in LEGIO VII GALBIANA fighting for the Flavian pretender Vespasianus killed an older soldier from LEGIO XXII loyal to the Emperor Vitellius, the older man turned out to be the young man's father.

The young soldier, left foreground, from LEGIO VII is equipped in the most up to date armour and equipment, his helmet is an iron Imperial Italic type based on a near complete example found in the river Rhine at Mainz. It is embellished with applied bronze strips and decorations in the form of eagles and shrines containing alters. An elaborate helmet like this could have been privately purchased, ironically with money from the soldier's father. He wears a laminated iron cuirass of Corbridge type and a leather belt with metal belt plates with quite a common design attached. The bronze belt apron, the fittings of which were often tinned, has lunate terminals with secondary smaller tear dropped pendants similar to those found in a hoard form Tekije, Serbia. His sword is of the latest straight sided type, called the *Pompeii* after examples found during excavations there, while the scabbard is also a design from amongst the large collection of military material discovered at Mainz. Finally he carries a straight sided plywood shield with bronze edging.

The older soldier from LEGIO XXII has armour and equipment that although serviceable was possibly being phased out amongst the Western legions by this date. The mail shirt with shoulder doubling that had changed little in over 200 years did not offer as much protection as the laminated armour, but was actually heavier. Around his waist he wears double belts worn 'cowboy' fashion and they are richly decorated with Niello inlaid plates. His curved sided shield was one of the earliest Imperial modifications to the old Republican shield, made lighter by simply removing the upper and lower rounded edges. The bronze Italic helmet he wears was rather a crudely finished specimen actually found on this battle site. Like the rest of his equipment his sword is the slightly old fashioned 'Mainz' type, long pointed with a tapering blade.

In the background is an Auxiliary infantryman not so differently equipped from that of the older legionary. The main difference being his flat oval shield more suitable for skirmishing duties and his stabbing spear or *hasta*. In addition he carries two lighter throwing javelins in the manner depicted on the Mainz column base. Compared with the legionary's helmets, his design is a veritable antique with an ancestry dating back to the Fifth century BC. It has been styled a legionary helmet but in view of its dated style could conceivably have been worn by an Auxiliary. Like the other bronze example it too was lost at this battle site. As a reflection of his non-Roman nature the Auxiliary wears a native type sword, like the one found at Hod Hill in Dorset. Beneath his mail shirt can be seen a fringed leather under garment.

All the soldiers wear dyed red military tunics of varying shades and the heavy leather hobnailed boots the *Caligae*. Visible in the background is a *Vexillum* flag type standard with a Capricorn motif, one of the insignia of LEGIO IIII MACEDONICA a participating unit in the battle.

Painting by Graham Turner.

---

arrangement underneath to allow flexibility of movement. This was an important step forward, but Von Groller's solution was to apply the metal strips to a leather jacket type garment.

By the 1960s, all the elements of the *Lorica Segmentata* girth hoops, hinge fittings and shoulder-straps had been gathered together by scholars but the true manner of their assembly was still misunderstood. Nor was the debate solely confined to the re-construction of Plate armour. A cause of division amongst academics to this day is the use of organic material, in particular leather as a form of body defence by the Romans. The grave stelae of Valerius Crispus for example is definitely not wearing a *Lorica Segmentata* and this armour was interpreted by early scholars as a leather *Muscled Cuirass*, as indeed Alma-Tadema had painted it. Around the thighs of Crispus are a number of rectangular strips and these were actually believed to be a pair of elaborate leather shorts!

Scholars like Robinson and the author and illustrator Peter Connolly interpreted these so called suits of leather armour as mail shirts. They argued convincingly that as most Roman sculpture had been originally brightly coloured, tedious details such as mail would originally have been picked out in paint, or even if mail had been rendered by the sculptor it had long since worn away, misleading historians into believing a smooth, leather surface had been intended in the first place. There are in fact a number of surviving reliefs which do show that Roman sculptors were capable on occasions of showing mail armour quite adequately.

For many years the most widely used example of a re-constructed Roman figure was that produced for the Grosvenor Museum, Chester, under the auspices of Dr Graham Webster as part of the Newstead gallery exhibits. Clearly there were many items of military equipment, helmets for instance, on which to base a reconstruction, but the assembly of the plate armour on this figure still owed much to Trajans Column.

Today it is popular to dismiss the efforts made by Hollywood film makers to recreate armour and

Opposite.

Top left.

Legionary *Vexilarius* and *Signifer* from the Adamklissi Tropaeum. Both wear mail shirts and knee length breeches. Neither has an animal skin head-dress normally associated with standard bearers.

Top right.

Cornicines from Second century sculpture. Top left from Trajan's Column and centre from the Adamklissi Tropaeum are both from the Dacian wars. Top right a *Cornicen* shown on the Column of Marcus Aurelius. This *Cornu* is similar to a very early Etruscan example.

Bottom left.

Aurelius Bitus, a *Cornicen* with LEGIO I ADIUTRIX based at Budapest c.200 AD.

Bottom right.

A *Tuba* depicted on a monument dating to the time of Marcus Aurelius.

equipment during the hey-day of the epic films in the 1950s and 60s. However it is obvious to anyone involved in re-enactment, how enormously influential these films are as regards the public's perception of Roman history. Like academics, movie researchers were to a great extent inspired by classical sculpture, and Roman soldiers from any period either Republican or the Empire looked like those on Trajan's Column. Muscled cuirasses and strip armour were everywhere!

Occasionally someone got their homework right and when actual archaeological evidence was used the film makers were on safer ground. Some credit must be given to the anonymous researcher who came up with a creditable version of a helmet, now classified as an Auxiliary type complete with its bowl reinforces,

A musical instrument, possibly of *Lituus,* from the Saalburg.

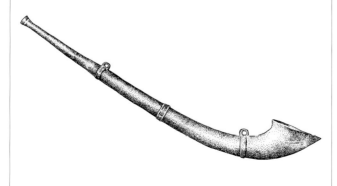

Reconstructed figure produced for the Grosvenor Museum, Chester in the 1950s. © Grosvenor Museum.

which appears in the early scenes of *Spartacus* (1960). Even more so since an exact re-construction of this helmet did not appear until Robinson's book *The Armour of Imperial Rome* published fourteen years later. This particular soldier's panoply was completed by a mail shirt worn under a leather garment decorated with a set of *Phalarae* awards. All of which was entirely consistent with current thinking. Unfortunately the script writers let everyone down by referring to this soldier as a 'Captain'!

Another correct detail was provided by the mounted escort to the character portrayed by Peter Ustinov. These cavalrymen were equipped exactly as interpreted at the time albeit in the leather jerkin and ridge helmets depicted on, yes you guessed it, Trajan's Column. Nevertheless to all who watch this film, the most remembered sequence is the spine tingling moment when the Legions of Crassus march over the hill to defeat the undisciplined hoards of Spartacus. Only the most hardened cynic can fail to be stirred.

The same use of mail shirts under leather arming doublets appeared in *The Fall of the Roman Empire* (1964) where a number of soldiers wear this

Even this production still from the film *Fall of the Roman Empire* captures a sense of atmosphere conjuring up an image of the Varus campaign in the forests of Germania. The Roman Infantry wear Auxiliary bronze helmets. © DCM 65.

combination. One particular force represented in this film was a unit of gladiators. In addition to the above armour they are also wearing a Triple disc *cuirass* worn by a bronze Samnite warrior from Sicily now in the Louvre Museum. This type of armour is also supported by archaeological finds including a splendid discovery from Alfedena in Italy. Marcus Aurelius, the Emperor in the film, played superbly by Alec Guiness, did in fact conscript gladiators in to his army so the film makers were quite correct in showing this, though whether they would have worn Samnite gladiator armour is another matter.

More surprising are the helmets worn by the Imperial Guards. These were not only based on an actual example but they were placed into their exact historical context, that is the latter half of the Second century AD. The helmet from Heddernheim classified now as a Cavalry 'Sports' type was a brave choice as it is not instantly recognisable as a Roman helmet, but this clearly reflected the general care and overall attention to detail rarely paid to in an historical movie.

It is not inconceivable that these helmets were worn by members of the Emperor's horse guards, similar ones do appear on their tombstones. Incidentally the Roman Forum set built in Spain for *The Fall of The Roman Empire* was not only one of, if not the largest film sets ever built, it is also the most authentic. An interesting point put forward in the movie was the idea that the armies of the Eastern Empire were equipped differently from those in the West. The uniform worn in the east was of a lighter more beneficial type suitable for a hot climate. More importantly for the viewer it provided a useful device to avoid confusion when the two armies fought each other. The film is also notable for probably the only depiction of the heavily armoured 'Cataphract' Cavalry, used by the Roman's Persian adversaries.

All things considered the best movie re-constructions of legionary armour appears in the early scenes of the Elizabeth Taylor version of *Cleopatra* (1963). Although inappropriate for the period of Julius Caesar, Caesar's Legionaries wear a *Lorica Segmentata* based on the evidence then available, complete with italic helmets and studded aprons and a leather undergarment beneath the *Lorica*. This latter feature is seen on sculpture from the 'Antonine' period and overall the uniform is almost of museum quality.

Cleopatra was also one of the first films to suggest that Roman soldiers wore red tunics. Prior to this most films had decided upon white tunics often with a red hem. The most famous example of this being *Ben-Hur* (1959) for which the costumes won an Oscar amongst its record breaking haul of eleven in total. Regrettably the military uniforms are in truth amongst the poorest recorded on film although leather arming doublets are worn under the armour.

Top right.
Reconstruction of a *Cornicen* and *Cornu*, First century AD. The *Cornu* is based on the example from Pompeii now in Naples Museum.

Bottom left.
An *Imaginifer* carrying an *Imago* or image of the Emperor based on Genialis who served with **COHORS VII RAETORUM**. Although in this instance the image is that of Vespasianus.

Bottom right.
Reconstructed *Vexillarius* and *Vexillum* of **LEGIO II AUGUSTA** First Century AD. The elaborate standard tip may be of the type used by *Beneficiarii* but could equally have belonged to standards of this kind. In keeping with other standard bearers or musicians the *Vexillarius* wears an animal skin, in this instance a wolf skin.

First Century cavalryman on a Grave Stelae from Cologne. The saddle horns are well illustrated as is the mail shoulder doubling and fastener. The helmet has the embossed hair design.

Opposite.
Top left.
Cavalrymen, probably members of the EQUITES SINGULARES AUGUSTI, on a Trajanic relief. One rider wears a mail shirt the other a scale shirt.

Top right.
Auxiliary infantry and cavalry in action from 'Trajans Column'.

Bottom left.
Numidian light cavalryman shown on Trajan's Column. An elite Numidian cavalry unit fought in Trajan's wars and their commander Lucius Quietus became a leading general and even an aspirant for the Imperial Throne. Numidians were skilled horsemen who rode without saddles or bridles. The unique ethnic hairstyle may be artistic licence.

Bottom right.
Two types of Third century cavalrymen from the extremes of the Empire. The un-armoured cavalryman is from a fresco at Dura-Europos while the armoured cavalryman from Chester wears the new longer style mail shirt.

Almost uniquely, *Cleopatra* features some Roman Marines during the naval battle of Actium. Their uniforms were actually based on the sculpture in the Vatican museum which shows a war galley and associated figures. That most famous of Roman military manoeuvres 'The Tortoise' is also included early on in the film. Perhaps out of deference to Admiral Agrippa it is, however, referred to as a Turtle! Almost certainly the Portonaccio Sarcophagus now in Rome's Museo Nazionale provided the origins for the leather *Lorica Segmentata* used in many of the lesser Italian epics. Helmets also from this source complete with their distinctive ring crests were often used and can be seen in the Franco Zefferelli TV epic *Jesus of Nazareth* (1976). The same production company released the less successful and well known sequel *AD Anno Domini* (1986) detailing the life and times of Christ's Disciples up until the reign of Nero. Although armour from *Jesus of Nazareth* was re-used some effort was made to introduce more accurate equipment. The scene of Caligula's army preparing for the invasion of

Column of reconstructed legionaries on the march.

Britain was perhaps the most memorable. Auxiliary soldiers wear helmets fashioned with the embossed hair design familiar from many monuments and archaeological finds. Archers in long flowing robes can also be spotted as well as an example of a *Coolus* type helmet. Meanwhile Caligula's camp is surrounded by a series of fortifications that would not have been out of place at Caesar's Siege of Alesia.

Any excuses that film or T.V. companies may have had before advances in archaeological reconstruction do not apply to those made more recently. The most glaring example being the lamentable effort recreating the series of events ending in the Siege of Masada. Entitled originally *Masada* (1982), it was released in a shortened cinema version *The Antagonists* after the book by Earnest. K. Gann on which the production was based. As a T.V. mini series it was a missed opportunity because there was plenty of scope to show in great detail military equipment and army life. Instead the film makers resorted to what would be termed today as a politically correct comment on the conflict between the Romans and Jews in First century Judaea. Experts on ancient artillery however will find much to amuse themselves with, if they even bother to watch.

In 1964 a major archaeological breakthrough occurred with the discovery of a hoard of Roman armour and a wealth of other material at the site of Corbridge near to Hadrian's Wall. The discovery was brought to the attention of H. Russell-Robinson, then Keeper of the Armouries at the Tower of London. Robinson's first attempts at reconstructing the fragments of *Lorica Segmentata* were hampered rather than helped by the influence of Trajan's Column. Also as it turned out there was more than one type of *Lorica Segmentata* included amongst the finds. Greater use could initially have been used of Robinson's own knowledge of oriental and medieval European armour and their reliance on flexible internal leather straps, which ultimately proved to be the key to his successful interpretation of the armour.

Unaware of this advance *The Ermine Street Guard* had been formed in 1972 by eight Gloucestershire men as part of a village pageant. *The Guard* had based their *Lorica* on a design which had appeared in Graham Webster's classic book *The Imperial Roman Army*. *The Guard* had been formed simply to perform an episode in the Pageant, with no intention on the part of the original members of continuing once the event was over. But with their interest awoken and

Reconstructed early Imperial legionaries.

having spent so much time and effort in preparing for the occasion the founding members decided to carry on with their research and improving the initial equipment.

Almost from the outset *The Guard* was fortunate to have made contact, quite by accident, with Russell Robinson. A local Gloucestershire archaeologist had taken one of *The Guard's Lorica* to a Roman Army course in Cardiff attended by Robinson. Robinson remarked that it was a pity that *The Guard* had gone to so much trouble to produce equipment that in the light of his recent work was incorrect. Other items of *The Guard's* reconstruction were also of dubious authenticity. It transpired that their helmets were of a hybrid design rather than based on any actual example, while their shields had been copied not unnaturally from the example on display in The Grosvenor Museum, a design that also bore no relation to any known Roman shield.

It is to *The Guard's* lasting credit that it was not deflated by these drawbacks, so early on in its conception, but instead set about correcting them. As the society and funds grew, the original items were gradually replaced, new ranks and armour types were added and the range of projects extended to include the construction of artillery machines and marching camp equipment. Perhaps the single most rewarding achievement in *The Guard's* history was to break down the scepticism initially encountered with the acknowledged experts in the field and to become accepted by these very experts .

For many years *The Guard* remained alone as Roman re-enactors, but from 1982 onwards there appeared other groups of varying quality. The majority, followed along the ground already broken by *The Guard* in adopting the First century AD as the period of study. There have however been some notable exceptions. In 1985, the Bavarian military historian Dr Marcus Junkelmann led a small re-created detachment on a 23 day march from Verona to Augsburg to celebrate the 2000th anniversary of that city's foundation. Junkelmann's group was equipped as Augustan Legionaries and Officers by the British armourer Michael Simkins, also author of the *Osprey* titles on the Roman Army. Primarily the group were formed for the duration of this single event, but like *The Guard* Junkelmann had developed an interest that was to continue long after the initial project. After the conclusion of the Augsburg march he turned his attention to re-creating a Roman cavalry unit. Both of Junkelmann's groups have carried out the role of the Roman soldier beyond the normal public displays of other societies to eating, sleeping, and training in Roman fashion.

An essential part of a cavalryman's equipment is his saddle. For many years it had been believed that the combination of a lack of stirrups and inadequate saddle had relegated the Roman cavalry to little more than a supporting role. This seemed barely conceivable in view of the sculptural evidence to the contrary, but positive proof was lacking. The story of how finds from Valkenburg and Vechten were interpreted and reconstructed by Peter Connolly are one of the positive achievements of re-enactment. Connolly's saddle has been put to the test by a number of experienced riders, not least during public displays by re-enactors. The secure seat provided by the four horns on the saddle have dramatically demonstrated that Romans had the capability of mounting shock tactics, including the use of a hand held lance without fear of being knocked out of the saddle on impact.

There have been a number of attempts by reconstruction groups to interpret the marching pack in use by the Roman armies. Most scholars and re-enactors agree that the method shown on Trajan's Column for carrying the pack on a large pole held high in the air, is most likely an artistic device to show

Opposite: top left and right. Top.
Camel warriors from Palmyra, the desert city state and ally of
Rome. Similar soldiers armed and equipped would have
formed the nucleus of Rome's camel riders. The only known
commander of Rome's single camel unit was himself a
Palmyrene.

Opposite: bottom.
Cavalry standard Bearers.
(left) Carminius Ingenuus of ALA I HISPANORUM from Worms.
(right) Flavinius of ALA GALLORUM PETRIANA from Hexham.

off the various piece of equipment the soldiers carried.
Practical research has demonstrated that the soldier
would require the use of both hands to balance the
pole and pack in this manner . Not only is that
impractical but all the entrenching implements
hanging from the bundle, would become a nuisance to
the carrier and also to his immediate comrades once
the march began. However many artistic
reconstructions including those by Ronald Embleton
and Peter Connolly have faithfully reproduced not
only the pack held aloft, but also include a number of
entrenching tools such as the pick-axe hanging from
the pole.

Re-enactors have concluded that if the pack is
attached to a shorter pole and held close to the back,
this can be easily kept in position with the minimum
of effort. Another plausible suggestion is that the
various pieces of equipment can even be carried on the
pickaxe (Dolabra) itself. As the pickaxe could be
described as being 'T' shaped it is not inconceivable
that this was mistaken by the Roman sculptors as a
separate wooden pole. Undoubtedly the Romans had
the technology to invent a back-pack similar to those
in use by more recent armies, but it was no doubt
considered it would damage or be damaged by the
moving action of the plate armour on the march.

Soldiers equipped with mail shirts would not
encounter this problem but Republican and early
Imperial troops would have been faced with another
difficulty. Shields of that period were much larger and
heavier than later Imperial counterparts. For their
reconstructions, the Junkelmann group invented an
elaborate harness to carry the shield on the back like a
pack. Any form of back-pack could clearly not be
carried in addition. Whether this was the reason why
the Romans never developed a marching pack is
something that will never be proved. Junkelmann's
system evidently worked, although it has been pointed
out that the soldier could be surprised and knocked
helpless like a turtle. When the shorter Imperial shield

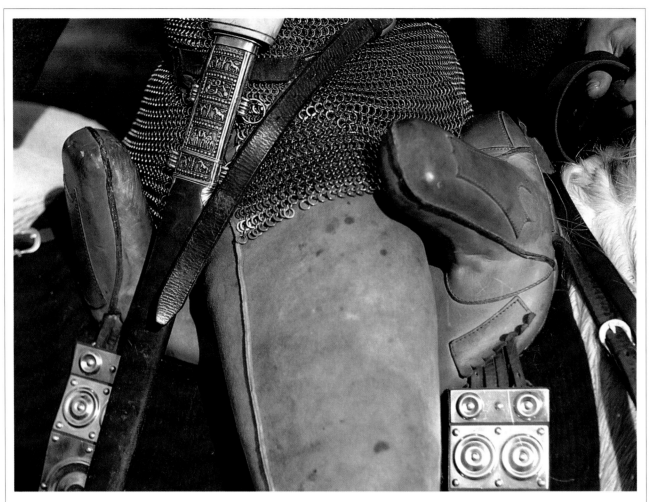

Reconstructed saddle showing how the two projecting horns on either side help to keep the rider in position.

is carried on the back in this manner re-enactors have found it bangs into the back of the legs. Therefore a method of carrying the shield by means of a simple shoulder strap, or basically carrying it in the normal manner, is adopted. With either method, a 'T' shaped pole with equipment can be balanced without too much difficulty, this includes carrying an extra *Pilum*. Ironically this was exactly the method proposed by the

Reconstruction of a Roman cavalry saddle by Peter Connolly.

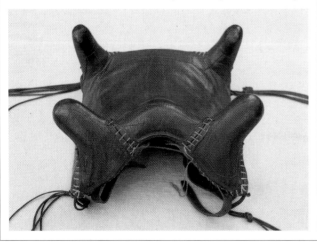

artist Amedee' Forestier in his book *The Roman army* published in 1927. While of course there is some debate over the exact amount and nature of equipment carried by the Romans, even the highest estimates are not demonstrably heavier than those of their modern equivalents.

When faced with a fully equipped and armoured re-enactor for the first time, many sharp eyed members of the public notice the sword is worn on the right, therefore the wrong side. Many people including several academics find it difficult to appreciate how the sword is drawn from such an awkward looking position. Indeed one theory was put forward which argued that the majority of swords discovered where in fact elaborate officers' swords intended for votive deposits not for battle. It was further suggested that swords longer than a blade 50.8cm in length could not be drawn and also would not be effective in the close quarter fighting favoured by the legionary. Finally it was claimed that all swords of this length must have belonged to the Auxilia where a greater degree of flexibility was required in battle.

Re-enactors of course find this all somewhat ludicrous, no problems whatsoever are encountered when drawing the sword from the right, even after a minimum of training. In fact swords in excess of this

One suggested method of sword attachment in the First century. The scabbard is tied to the belt by means of a leather thong passed through the suspension rings. The scabbard plate is a reinterpretation of the evidence from 'Long Windsor' by Martin White of *The Ermine Street Guard*, based on a find from Valkenburg.

Modern interpretation of how the Gladius was drawn as suspended from the right.

length up to and including the long Celtic *Spatha* type can even be drawn. By placing the sword in this position the Romans were able to withdraw their swords without resorting to moving their shield aside, a process which would be required if the sword was worn on the other side. A tight formation could therefore be maintained as the Romans closed with the enemy, also they did not needlessly expose their bodies to their opponents missile fire.

The solution to the seemingly awkward position employed is the relationship of the sword scabbard to the belt. Roman grave stelae in particular Auxiliary ones from the First century, provide one clue. While the dagger scabbard is clearly held on by a system of frog leathers, no such arrangement is shown for the sword scabbard. Instead the sword belt passes behind and between the two sets of rings on either side of the scabbard. A simple leather thong crossed behind the belt and through the rings would secure the scabbard

in this position. Alternatively a method frequently employed by the legionaries is to suspend the scabbard from a long *Baldric*. The *Baldric* strap is split into two as it approaches the two scabbard rings on the wearer's left. Each strap is then attached to the suspension rings on the scabbard which is placed below the waist belt. The waist belt in turn is passed over the *Baldric* strap holding it firmly in position against the body enabling the sword to be drawn. If further proof be needed watch the film *Fall of the Roman Empire* where even Stephen Boyd draws his sword from the right while mounted on a horse!

Most of the major Roman re-enactment groups have now gone beyond the re-construction of the basic arms and armour of the soldiers, branching into other areas of military hardware such as artillery and field equipment. For many years it had been the intention of *The Ermine Street Guard* to produce an eight man leather *Contuburnium* Tent based on designs produced by the archaeologist I.A Richmond in the 1920s. However finds of leather panels positively identified as belonging to tents, were discovered in the 1980s which raised doubts about Richmond's reconstructions. Finally in 1987 Robin Birley discovered a significant find of leather panels during excavations at Vindolanda. These panels proved to be from a leather tent that was of a more practical nature than thought previously. Not only did it provide some standing room but even with eight men inside there would be space for the soldiers' equipment.

The Guard's *Contuburnium* tent was constructed after consultation with Carol Van Driel-Murray an expert in Roman leather work together with Sue Winterbottom from Carlisle Archaeological Unit, who had both worked on the finds of leather material. Not only did the construction consist of seventy seven goat skins but the two re-enactors involved in this task, Tim Haines and Bill Mayes faced the daunting job of stitching over one hundred yards of seams. This one example demonstrates the single minded effort that is so often required when attempting any reconstruction of Roman equipment. It also illustrates how close co-operation between re-enactors and archaeologists can have beneficial results.

Reconstructed cavalryman in sports equipment, late First century AD. The horse chamfron is based on two examples possibly made by the same craftsmen which were found at Newstead and Vindolanda. The parade helmet is a reconstruction of the Ribchester helmet now in the British Museum.

Armour and Helmets

Mail (*Lorica Hamata*)

Many people are surprised to discover that the Romans wore mail shirts as a protective garment. Mail is more often associated with the later medieval periods. Indeed it is not unknown for Roman re-enactors in mail shirts to be labelled Vikings! In fact mail was invented long before the Roman period. But while the origins of this form of defence may be in dispute the Romans themselves believed it was the Celts who had invented it, and almost certainly it was through contact with the Celts that it was introduced into the Roman Army.

Mail is made from interlocking one iron ring with four others. The simplest method of construction is to have alternative rows of punched out rings from sheet metal interlocked with wire rings which are either butted or riveted. This initial process of manufacture requires a high degree of skill, also making it an expensive procedure. However once a shirt is finished it is largely self cleaning, due to the rubbing action of the rings, requiring a minimum of maintenance. Therefore it is quite possible that mail shirts were passed down from generation to generation.

The Romans adopted two types of mail shirt with and without shoulder reinforces. The latter type mainly seem to have been worn by the Auxilia but there is some evidence they were used by the legionaries as well. The grave stelae of Castricius Victor a legionary from Aquincum shows him wearing one of these shirts. The design of the shirts with shoulder reinforcement echo the stiffened linen *cuirasses* worn in classical Greek armies. Shoulder doubling appears to have been attached at the rear just below the arm holes. The doubling was then brought forward over the shoulders and tied to the front of the shirt by means of a chest fastener, of which there are a variety of different designs.

Modern re-enactors have found that if the doubling has a leather backing this helps to keep the shoulder straps from splaying while also keeping out rain. All forms of armour worn by the Romans prove to be heavy and ultimately tiring to the wearer. A mail shirt weighs about 10kgs and is perhaps the most comfortable as it fits the form of the body, in addition by wearing a belt, some of the weight is transferred from the shoulders. One aspect of a mail shirt that becomes apparent to those who wear it as opposed to plate armour is that the wearer is able to take deeper breaths. A noticeable feature on monuments like Trajan's Column is that legionary musicians such as the Cornicen are still equipped in mail shirts even after plate armour had been widely adopted. Perhaps due to similar circumstances, Standard Bearers also wear mail shirts on many monuments. In their case the obvious requirement of keeping the arms raised holding a standard, would be more comfortable in a mail shirt.

Republican mail shirts reached down to mid thigh but those of the early Empire were shorter, fitting to just below the waist. To make up for this lack of protection, strips, probably of leather called *Pteruges*, appear on many sculptures at the shoulders and around the hips. These *Pteruges* were almost certainly part of an undergarment worn beneath the mail shirt. In the past, artists' reconstructions often depicted Roman soldiers wearing a leather garment over the mail shirt, a practice not unknown in medieval European and Oriental armies. Support for such a thing happening in Roman times comes from Caesar's account of the Siege of Dyrrachium when as added protection against arrows some of his soldiers effected to make padded garments out of fabric, felt or hide. Garments just like these were used by the Crusaders and on one occasion, after being showered by Saracen arrows, they were described as looking like porcupines. That Caesar specifically mentions such a garment being made would seem to suggest, that it was an emergency measure and that normally it wasn't worn . But while mail provides adequate protection against slashing sword strokes, it is susceptible to

50 Armour and Helmets

Detail of a scale hood from the Third century AD. This reconstruction owes its inspiration to the battle of Ebenezer fresco in the synagogue at Dura Europos. This fresco appears to reflect contemporary details in armour and equipment although it is not always clear whether scale or mail armour was intended.

Reconstructed mail fastener based on a find from the fortress of Usk.

stabbing thrusts or puncturing by arrows.

Recently tests have proved that arrow heads of the types used in ancient times will pierce mail fairly easily. If the soldier was not killed outright, the arrow would almost certainly force rings from the shirt into the wound, with potentially fatal results. Even if the soldier was only slightly wounded he would face the agonising situation of having to have his mail removed, while the arrow was still in his body, so the wound could be treated. Modern day historians and some re-enactors therefore believe an extra garment was worn, not over the mail but beneath it. Perhaps this is the *Subarmalis* mentioned in the Vindolanda writing tablets. Later Roman writers also refer to a

Opposite.
Reconstruction of a Third century soldier based mainly on evidence from Dura Europos. The ring buckle and belt terminals appear on the sculpture of Mucianus from Apamea.

Thoracomachus which may describe the same type of garment, as this too apparently was worn under armour.

Previous interpretations of the apparently smooth form of armour worn by many Roman soldiers on sculptural monuments described this as leather armour or, as mentioned before, leather worn over mail. A hatched effect which appeared to peep out from beneath this smooth garment on many tombstones was therefore believed to be mail. This interpretation took no account of the fairly widespread practice by the Romans of rendering their sculptured monuments in coloured paints. This would have included many of the military tombstones as well and in some cases, especially in the carved lettering on these monuments, traces of colour survives. A lot of tedious detail could well have been added in paint rather than chiselled and mail would have been an obvious subject to treat in this manner.

At first glance many of the figures on Trajan's Column appear to be wearing smooth jerkins, but close inspection reveals that in this case the sculptors did attempt to represent mail with very fine chisel

Celtic warrior of the late First century BC, from Avignon. Apart from the large neck *torque* he could easily be identified as a Roman soldier and shows the strong Celtic influence on Roman equipment.

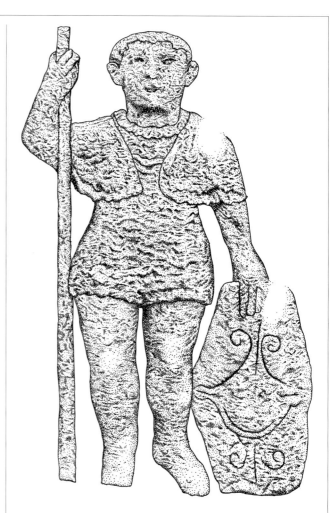

Celtic relief of the God Mars, First century AD. The mail shirt with shoulder doubling and front fastener were both adapted by the Romans.

marks. Time and pollution have worn most of this away but remarkably casts made of the monument in the Nineteenth century have preserved many details that would otherwise have been lost. Wearing an undergarment beneath mail does have obvious advantages, in that it would provide extra protection against arrows or stabbing thrusts. Other practical uses are that it helps to keep the woollen tunic cleaner as it is protected from the mail and would make it easier for the soldier to actually put the mail on in the first place.

To combat the short stabbing spears encountered in the wars against the Germanic tribes, plate armour may have gradually been introduced as the mail was found wanting. Some First century tombstones nevertheless appear to show legionaries still wearing this armour suggesting mail was not phased out entirely. Also it is a widely held belief that as the legionaries converted to plate armour, their old mail shirts were passed on to Auxiliaries. A strange irony that the supposedly inferior Auxilia were equipped with the more expensive form of armour. Another line

of thought implies that the use of mail remained widespread in the Eastern half of the Empire as it would have been cooler to wear than plate armour. Indeed finds of *Lorica Segmentata* are rare but increasing. The balance of excavation and research is heavily weighed in favour of the West. The lack of evidence therefore may simply be a result of this, rather than anything else. Ironically it would be on the Eastern frontier that Roman soldiers wearing mail would face their greatest threat, from the arrow firing Parthians and later Persians. After all it was the mounted archers of the Parthian army which had destroyed a Roman army at Carrhae in 53 BC.

While Trajan's Column presents us with a picture of all Roman legionaries wearing plate armour, the Adamklissi Tropaeum erected to commemorate the same wars tells a different story. Here the legionaries wear mail and scale armour rather than the plate which does not appear at all. Many historians believe this monument, although cruder, was probably carved by sculptors more familiar with the frontier army than those who erected the public monuments in Rome.

Cavalrymen from the column of Marcus Aurelius. The top figure wears a mail shirt, his fellow cavalrymen a scale shirt. The spear held over arm is a common method depicted on sculpture. The top figure is little changed from the figures on 'Trajans Column' eighty years earlier. The strap on the shield is also a regular feature in Roman sculpture but is not supported by any archaeological finds.

Thus it is conceivable that the Adamklissi Tropaeum is a truer reflection of the Roman army, at least in the Dacian Campaign of Trajan, than what we are normally led to believe. What is certain is that mail as a form of defence continued to be used throughout and beyond the Roman period.

Scale Armour *(Lorica Squamata)*

Like mail, scale armour pre-dated the Roman period and had a very long history. Scale armour appears to have been invented in the East, it was known to the Assyrians, and remained a popular form of armour there. Judging by the sculptural evidence, with the possible exception of the Auxiliary infantry, scale armour in its various forms was worn by every class of Roman soldier including the Emperor. The reason for

Legionary in marching order in northern Britain, 160 - 180 AD

In the painting opposite, as much as possible of the legionary's equipment is based on finds from the major fort site at Newstead in the Scottish borders, abandoned around 180 AD. Overall the equipment, especially the body armour found at Newstead and the helmet based on one from Thielenhofen, are simpler than those in the First century AD, lacking a lot of the elaborate but unnecessary detail of the earlier period. This is particularly noticeable in the belt and apron which is shorter than before perhaps because leather *Pteruges* are worn. Similar strips belonging to an undergarment, probably slightly padded, can be seen on a stone carving at Croy Hill in Scotland.

The sword is now suspended from a scabbard slide in the form of a dolphin, rather than the suspension rings used before. The scabbard chape shown here was amongst the Newstead finds. This soldier supports a ring *Pommel* sword, both this and the scabbard style were probably introduced into the Roman army by the Sarmatians. It must be pointed out that no swords of this type have yet been found in Britain, however Sarmatian cavalry were posted to Britain close to this period so the possibility cannot be ruled out entirely. A *Pilum* tip discovered at Newstead shows this weapon was still in use at this time. While probably not 'regulation' issue the soldier has adopted the practice of wearing a type of leg protector common amongst outdoor labourers and huntsmen.

The Roman marching pack was suspended probably from a 'T' shaped pole or even one of the tools such as the pickaxe. It included some of the equipment shown here. In camp construction the soldier would use the axe and pickaxe. Also depicted is the enigmatic 'Turf cutter' named more after its likeness to the modern garden edging tool rather than its known use by the army. The other iron tool is a 'reaping' hook used to cut ears of corn. All these tools were found at Newstead with the exception of the sheath used to protect the axe head. Essential wooden tools for the erection of tents were the tent peg and mallet head also found at Newstead, however the stake probably used for camp defences is based on finds from Germany.

All the metal vessels and implements used for cooking, eating and drinking were excavated at Newstead, including the rare metal flask, although a better preserved example was found in Germany. A number of knives were found on the site as was the small two edged saw and the two sided iron file. These latter implements remind us that a legionary was something of an all round craftsman as well as a fighting soldier. A cloak could be kept in the pack as well as other spare clothes. Cloaks were held in place by brooches and the type shown here is a *Penannular,* which in overall design was actually pre-Roman.

When not in action the shield would be covered in a leather goat skin cover tied with a draw string, fixed to the front of which could be an appliqué panel, with the unit name picked out in open-work. Wickerwork baskets would be used in camp construction for earth moving as well as carrying items of equipment. The leather boots from Newstead are different to the First century styles of boot, and have more in common with heavy duty civilian footwear, perhaps evidence of a change in supply policy. Painting by Graham Turner.

this is not hard to understand, a well made scale shirt can be extremely attractive.

A shirt consists of a number of bronze or iron pieces which could be of a variety of sizes, with either rounded or pointed lower edges. The scales were then strengthened by being connected into rows, which overlapped taking the form of fish scales or tiles on a roof. Finally the scales were then sewn onto a fabric backing garment Additional strengthening could also be provided by an extra lining of straw between the scales and the fabric. Various other methods could be used to make the scales either stronger or more aesthetically pleasing, an embossed ridge down the centre of each scale for instance would strengthen it. Sculptured renditions of this technique give the appearance of feathered plumage, like that of an Eagle, a particularly appropriate device for a Roman. The appearance of bronze scale could be further enhanced by tinning every alternative scale silver, leaving the others their remaining brass colour. An equal result would be achieved by using bronze and iron scales intermixed in a similar manner.

A basic scale shirt would be infinitely easier to construct and repair than mail and thus was a cheaper alternative. Therefore it is easy to appreciate its wide use by the Roman army, but the apparent absence of this armour in representations of Auxiliary infantry is somewhat surprising. In overall shape a scale shirt was generally close to that of a mail shirt, they could even on occasions have the shoulder doubling similar to the Republican and early Imperial mail. Unlike mail, scale is more rigid and faced with this lack of flexibility re-enactors have one immediate problem, how to put it on.

Two suggestions have been put forward and these have both been put into practice. On the shirts with shoulders, a rear neck opening is best and for those which have arm extensions a side opening is used. Neither method can of course be reliably confirmed by Roman sculpture which generally shows the figure frontally. Both procedures would require some assistance in putting on the shirt as indeed would the more familiar plate armour. Despite the many reservations of modern commentators who envisage

Top left and right.

Two First century AD, sculptures on tombstones showing the retention of mail as body armour by legionaries. Both carry *Pila* **and wear** *Pteruges*. **The sculptors have represented helmets but without obscuring the faces of the deceased. The left figure is Caius Valerius Crispus from LEGIO VIII AUGUSTA holding a curved rectangular shield with a decorated boss possibly representing a bull, the Legions emblem. Caius Castricus Victor from LEGIO II ADIUTRIX on the other hand has an oval one apparently with an boss depicting the head of the Gorgon Medusa. The baldric strap of Castricus is studded, a feature which also appears on portrait paintings from Egypt.**

the chaos and confusion this would cause during a surprise attack, it would seem this was an unavoidable and an acceptable risk the Romans were prepared to take. Perhaps this explains the almost obsessive care and attention that was paid by the Romans to their armies on the march and with the fortifications to their marching camps.

Tests have concluded that scale offered a greater degree of protection from arrows than mail, especially in those areas where the surface was doubled. The use of this doubling seems to have been popular with the cavalry, although the use of scale as a preferred choice of armour for the cavalry is surprising. By all historical accounts, cavalrymen would not normally be expected to receive blows to the shoulder areas as they were generally used against infantry. Furthermore if scale has a weakness it is that it can be ruptured by an upward thrust, which would be made easier if the wearer was in an elevated position, such as on a horse.

On the Adamklissi Tropaeum, scale shirts are depicted together with the characteristic strip type undergarment. In this case it would appear this garment had been modified and instead of a layer of single strips these have been replaced by layers of two or even three strips. Another feature which initially appears on a First century cavalry tombstone is the attachment of two small plates on the chest reaching to just below the neck and extending towards the shoulders. While this could be seen as a badly attempted representation of shoulder doubling, an alternative explanation is that this is the ancestor of the metal breast plates that appeared in the Third century.

Breast plates are often embossed and die stuck, in appearance they are not dissimilar to the breast plates on a *Lorica Segmentata* in that they are cut away in a curve to fit around the wearer's neck. They are attached by turning-pins and slots at the centre. These plates were then riveted to the scale shirt behind.

Trajanic legionary equipped for the Dacian wars as depicted on the Adamklissi Tropaeum. The scale shirt laminated arm defences and leather *Pteruges* are in marked contrast to the sculptures of Trajan's Column.

Robinson believed these plates protected a neck opening which was now at the front, but also that they belonged to infantry and cavalry parade armour. However elaborate equipment does not necessarily mean it was solely used for display.

Plate Armour *(Lorica Segmentata)*

Apart from the *Muscled Cuirass*, the strip plate armour known today as *Lorica Segmentata* is the type of body defence most often associated with the Roman soldier. *Lorica Segmentata* has been used by artists, sculptors and film makers when depicting soldiers of any period in Roman history. In fact this type of armour was only in use for about two hundred years compared to other forms of armour which were in continual use.

Scholars have often maintained that the *Lorica Segmentata* was a development introduced to rapidly replace the huge loss of mail armour as a result of the Varus disaster of AD 9. The three legions lost on this occasion needed to be rapidly replaced and equipped, both mail and scale armour would have been time

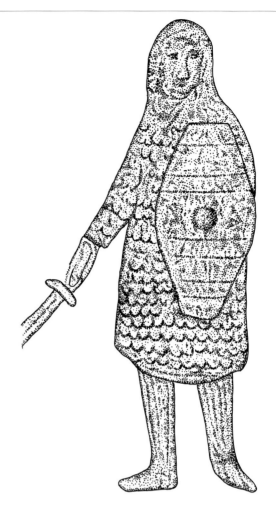

Figure in scale armour of the Third century AD Dura Europos synagogue fresco. The soldier appears to have a reed shield but most striking is the hood of scale armour.

consuming forms of defence to re-equip replacement troops. Whereas mail and scale were pre-Roman inventions, plate armour would appear to have been a purely Roman invention. A recent intriguing theory put forward the suggestion that *Lorica Segmentata* developed from gladiatorial armour. Segmented arm defences are indeed a common feature of gladiatorial figures both in sculpture and other two dimensional forms of art, but less well known are the armoured Gladiators known as *Crupellarii.*

In a number of instances Gladiators fought alongside the Legions but on one particular occasion during the revolt of 'Sacrovir' in Gaul in 21 AD, Gladiators including *Crupellarii* fought against the Romans. The *Crupellarii* were described by the historian Tacitus as being totally encased in iron armour and made as much impression on the Romans as the armoured Cataphract Cavalry of the Parthians and Persians also did. The armour of the *Crupellarii* proved as effective against the javelins and swords of the Romans as archery tests on *Lorica Segmentata* suggest it would have been. Most blows simply

Front and rear views of reconstructed legionary equipment based on finds from Britain and Germany.

deflected off the curved surfaces. In the end the Roman troops resorted to using their field tools to smash open the armour of these Gladiators and this was after these Gladiators were immobilised by pitchforks and poles and left helpless on the ground.

As anyone who wears a reconstructed *Lorica Segmentata* would know it is not so heavy it would render its wearer immobile, in fact research suggests actual Roman armour would have been lighter than most modern reconstructions. This would suggest that the armour worn by the *Crupellarii* was heavier than that adopted by the Roman Army. Whether or not the Romans did base their armour on that of the *Crupellarii* remains uncertain, but the general study of Gladiatorial equipment is perhaps worthy of more academic attention. Recent archaeological evidence has however dramatically altered historians opinion of the date when the *Lorica Segmentata* was introduced. Excavations at a site in Germany put forward as the scene of Varus's famous defeat of AD. 9 uncovered fragments of an early form of *Lorica Segmentata* proving it was already in existence by that date.

Sculpture suggests the existence of a number of variants in the type of segmented armour worn, a situation confirmed by archaeology. The efficiency of hook and strap fastenings always provided teething troubles, which the Romans never seemed to have completely ironed out. Any dramatic movement on the part of the wearer such as that expected in a battle may lead to wear or breakages of some sort. This is supported by the multifarious number of hinges and fittings found on Roman sites. Further more the internal leathers are vulnerable to deterioration from sweat and heat which can often result in kthe need for complete repair.

The most effective elements of the *Cuirass* are the girth straps and curved shoulder plates. These deflect most blows from swords or arrows not only due to their curved surfaces but also the fact that the armour was left soft which tended to absorb any impact. If provided with a padded undergarment the soldier would in all likelihood receive only severe bruising at worst.

Bishop has proposed that the existence of an undergarment would not only raise the armour off the shoulders but also alter the slant of the front plates to an angle of 90°. On all reconstructions these front plates tend to cross over behind the other if worn without a padded undergarment. This would give the

Roman soldier the appearance of an American footballer, an effect further enhanced if any form of protective covering was worn over the armour. If we are to believe Trajan's Column, *Lorica Segmentata* was by that date the standardised equipment of the legionary soldier. As pointed out earlier other monuments do exist which show mail remained the equipment of some legionaries while *Lorica Segmentata* does not appear at all on the Adamklissi Tropaeum.

The Corbridge armour proved to be Hadrianic in date, slightly later than previously believed. As expected the areas where most damage was likely to occur was to the shoulder pieces. All the remains of these pieces amongst the Corbridge finds showed evidence of breakages, and this may have been one reason why the armour had been discarded. Although no complete examples were recovered from the Corbridge site the finds proved to be fragments from three different iron sheet *Cuirasses*. Traces also existed of the internal leather straps which made this armour articulate. The three suits of armour seemed to show a pattern of evolution which gradually reduced the number of external leather straps and buckles replacing them with metal hooks and loop fastenings.

Reconstructed Third century AD scale shirt with front fastening breast plate.

During the middle of the Second century AD it is conceivable these earlier designs were being replaced by another less complex one. Armed with his knowledge of the Corbridge finds, Robinson turned his attention to fragments of armour found at the fort of Newstead in Scotland. From this evidence he produced a more workmanlike suit of armour that was an improvement on the earlier Corbridge types. There was less reliance on buckles and hinges than previous examples and tended to confirm his evolutionary theory put forward earlier. While inevitably some doubt has been cast on this reconstruction, in particular its lack of flexibility compared with the Corbridge types, it remains the most convincing version yet put forward.

Contemporary sculpture implies the existence of further modifications. One particular example involved the extension of girth strips from the waist up to the neck. Rather than experiment to see if this were

Embossed breastplates on scale armour like this reconstructed example, were believed to be a type of parade equipment. However they may simply be a new development which protected both the neck openings of scale shirts and replaced the chest fasteners of mail shirts. Deities like the Hercules figure depicted here were popular subjects on these breast plates.

possible, modern re-enactors have tended to agree with Robinson that this was merely artistic license.

Lorica Segmentata disappears from the sculptural record after the early Third century, although there is some archaeological evidence to support the existence of this armour after this date. Today there is general agreement amongst historians that this form of armour did not survive long in to the Third century.

A common practice amongst scholars has been the many attempts to standardise or stereotype the Roman army and its soldiers. This has been no more apparent than in the study of forts and fortresses and the assumption that they were all built to the same design. These forts housed a corresponding number of men or type of soldier relevant presumably to a particular location, that is, Auxiliaries in an Auxiliary fort. As our knowledge and understanding has increased these beliefs have been challenged, even discounted. In the same way it had been believed that *Lorica Segmentata* was the sole preserve of the Roman citizen legionary and would not have been used by the native Auxiliaries. Recently some scholars have doubted this, in particular on the grounds that the majority of *Lorica Segmentata* fittings were not found on legionary sites but actually in Auxiliary forts. Was it possible therefore that Auxiliaries too were equipped with this armour? Other evidence seemed to point that way. For both *Pilum* heads and possibly artillery bolts considered to be exclusively legionary weapons were also discovered on Auxiliary sites. While it may have been technologically possible for Auxiliaries to equip themselves in legionary equipment and there may have been tactical reasons for them doing so, all the other sources of evidence contradict this theory.

The existence of battle groups composed of mixed force of legionaries and Auxiliaries now termed Vexillations is a fairly recently recognised phenomenon. That similar mixed forces could later form the basis of many permanent garrisons of what are termed Auxiliary forts is a distinct possibility. This

The Centurion Timokles on a sculpture from Epidaurus complete with his horse and servant.

Fragment of a stone relief from the Adamklissi Tropaeum showing a muscled cuirass. Part of a mounted rider can be seen on the cuirass as well as a decorated sword scabbard attached to an elaborate belt. Two layers of scallops decorated with leaves and rosettes overlay the leather or linen fringed *Pteruges*.

would certainly account for the wide dispersal of legionary armour. Many forts and fortresses seem to have been little more than transit or training camps not unlike army barracks today. It is probably wrong to see a fort simply held by one particular unit at full strength waiting to be attacked by the enemy. The difference between legionary and Auxiliary equipment is emphasised by sculpture and literature. While there did exist one *COHORS SCUTATA C.R.* there is no evidence to suggest they wore legionary armour unless mail counts in that category or that the shield carried by this unit was a curved legionary type. Although Trajan's Column may display the distinction between the two categories of troops as a simplistic device for the citizens of the capitol, the difference is also maintained on the grave stelae of the frontier armies. A relief from Arlon in Luxembourg at first glance appears to show Auxiliary cavalry wearing *Lorica Segmentata* shoulder pieces. This is not corroborated by any other source. They could even represent legionary cavalry as there is no evidence at all for their particular uniform, if indeed they had one.

Compared with other forms of armour, *Lorica*

Segmentata was easier to construct and was presumably a cheaper alternative to mail and scale. Offset against this was the degree of regular maintenance that would be required and the effort on the part of the individual soldier to keep it clean. As it never appears to have been worn by anyone other than the front line soldier it was obviously appreciated for its defensive qualities.

Lamellar Armour

Lamellar armour like mail and scale armour had a long ancestry dating back to at least Assyrian times and was common amongst the nobility of the Parthian, Palmyrene and Persian Empires. Unlike scale armour from which it was developed, lamellar was laced to its backing in rigid horizontal rows. The individual pieces were longer and slimmer than those used in a scale shirt providing an even stiffer form of defence. Alternatively some lamellar could be of rawhide rather than metal. Examples of rawhide lamellar armour

Reconstruction of a leather undergarment showing the strips known as *Pteruges* at waist and shoulders.

lacquered either red or black and laced together with red leather thongs was discovered during excavations at Dura-Europos. Robinson believed this was from thigh defences worn by cavalrymen in the manner of cowboys chaps.

Judging from the archaeological evidence, although lamellar was widely known throughout the Empire it was not used in any great quantity, Robinson suggested it would mainly have been the equipment of units with Eastern origins. No complete reconstructions of this armour exist and Robinson's own research was based on his knowledge of later examples of lamellar that continued to be used as a form of defence in the East up to the Nineteenth century. Lamellar armour for both man and horse was discovered by British explorers in Tibet in 1904. The basic design of this Tibetan armour was similar to surviving fragments in use by the Sassanid Persians in the Fourth century AD.

Comparable to scale, lamellar armour was also produced in more intricate versions. Fragments of very fine lamellar armour was discovered at Corbridge. This armour may well have belonged to an officer of a nearby Eastern Auxiliary unit or an ordinary soldier with very expensive taste. In common with other types of armour, lamellar armour also came with shoulder doubling and leather or linen *pteruges* at the shoulders and around the waist. Statues of Palmyrene Gods are a good source of evidence for the design of these cuirasses which often show a strong Hellenistic influence.

Muscled Cuirass

With the possible exception of the *Lorica Segmentata*, the muscled cuirass is undoubtedly the most easily recognised form of Roman armour. This is due in no small measure to its continual and widespread representation throughout the entire Roman period in sculpture and art. Muscled cuirasses were common in the Greek and Hellenistic world and wealthy Romans in the early Republic would also have been familiar with them. It is therefore somewhat ironic to discover that not a single example form the Roman period has ever been recovered.

It was often believed in the past that cuirasses could have been made from moulded leather, this would certainly account for the lack of any surviving evidence. A more likely explanation is that despite

Reconstructed First century AD apron and terminals.

their popularity with sculptors, who depicted all classes of Roman troops wearing them, they were as far as one can tell the exclusive preserve of the senior officers. Surviving examples from earlier periods display a high degree of workmanship. Their simplistic attention to anatomical detail is in marked contrast to the over elaborate and vulgar decoration which appears to have been characteristic of the Roman type.

There are two patterns of muscled cuirass shown on monuments. The first is high waisted and parallels

Top.
Reconstruction of a late Second, early Third century cavalryman in scale armour with breast plate and strip *Pteruges* at the shoulder.

Bottom left.
A Roman Auxiliary engages a Dacian warrior armed with a long handled *Falx*. This relief from the Adamklissi Tropaeum clearly illustrates how the *Falx* could be used to get around the Roman shield.

Bottom right.
This Roman Legionary complete with arm guards deals successfully with a Dacian opponent armed with a *Falx*. A detail from the Adamklissi Tropaeum.

those which were probably used by Greek cavalry. A particular fine example of this type is the statue of Drusus in the Cagliari Museum. As a member of the Imperial family one would expected to see Drusus in a highly fanciful suit of armour, instead the opposite is the case. Drusus was well known as an experienced soldier who died of wounds on active service. He is represented in a functional and therefore believable cuirass as befitting a respected military figure. Almost uniquely in officers' panoplies, Drusus also has a helmet, showing strong Hellenistic influences, not simply a standard *Attic* helmet familiar from countless monuments.

The second type of cuirass rests further down on the hips with a curved extension at the bottom. This would be an extremely inflexible and uncomfortable form of armour if the wearer was mounted on a horse. Some of the sculptural examples extend to cover the shoulders and upper arms. This would be acceptable if the armour was of either mail of scale but any form of movement would clearly be impossible in a rigid cuirass.

Both surviving Hellenistic examples and some sculptures show the method of fastening was by means of hinges or rings which were tied up at the sides. Additionally straps extend over the shoulders and these are tied to rings piercing both nipples on the breast plate. Nipples on Hellenistic Bronze cuirasses are made of silver. In common with other types of armour the evidence suggest an undergarment worn beneath the muscled cuirass. The best example of this comes from a statue in the Museo delle Terme in Rome. What appears to be a leather arming doublet with scalloped edges and *Pteruges* attached is draped over a tree trunk.

Pteruges often descend from the arm opening and extend from beneath the scalloped edging, providing a degree of protection to the upper thighs. Frequently both scalloped edge and *Pteruges* have either extra decoration such as embossed metal plates and designs. The *Pteruges* themselves often have a fringed edging. Sometimes the scalloped edging is doubled or occasionally trebled. In such circumstances the P*teruges* are disposed with all together, as shown on the grave stelae of T. Exomnius Mansuetus, an Auxiliary prefect. Mansuetus wears a cuirass which extends over the shoulders. It is quite possible this is artistic licence on the part of the sculptor replacing more utilitarian, practical but less heroic forms of armour such as mail or scale.

Limb Armour
The most famous depictions of defence for the exposed limbs of soldiers are those from the Tropaeum Adamklissi commemorating the Dacians wars. The Roman fighting stance with the left leg forward and the right sword arm extended from behind the shield was no doubt vulnerable to the murderous scythe like weapon known as the *Falces* wielded by the Dacians. On the Adamklissi monument some legionaries are graphically illustrated wearing leg defences, greaves O*creae* and armguards *manicae* on the right arm. These have initially been seen as an isolated counter measure against the number of casualties inflicted by the *Falces*. It is not generally suggested that all legionaries were thus equipped, as presumably not all Dacians used *Falces*. Only a proportion of Roman troops would be required to wear limb defences and could be used whenever Dacians equipped when *Falces* appeared.

Greaves are seen as one of the unique distinguishing features of a Centurion's uniform, but apart from the Adamklissi reliefs another sculpture from Alba Iulia may also show an ordinary infantryman wearing one. A plain greave of the type shown on the Adamklissi monument was recovered from the fort at Kastell Kunzing, unfortunately some Centurions' greaves also appear to have been plain so this does not confirm their more generalised usage. Laminated arm defences in contrast do not seem to have been confined to the Dacian wars. Finds from Newstead and Carnuntum confirm their use in other theatres of operations. The possibility also exists, that other materials were used to construct limb defences. A complete greave for example made from layers of thick linen was recovered from Dura Europos 2nd, leather greave lining was discovered at Vindonissa. Robinson reconstructed the fragments from Newstead as thigh armour but this has been doubted recently and the suggestion that it is part or parts of arm defences is more likely.

This type of defence is also shown on the tombstone of Sex Valerius Severus, a legionary from LEGIO XXII PRIMIGENIA based at Mainz. It is also common on numerous gladiatorial reliefs, from which source it probably originated. Apart from the fact that they were fixed internally on to leather straps in the same manner as the *Lorica Segmentata*, the exact material and its construction is far from certain, fixed laminated plates down the entire length of the arm would severely restrict flexibility. In medieval times a separate plate known as a *counter* was worn over the elbow joint which greatly facilitated movement. A defensive plate equivalent to a *counter* does not appear on any of the Adamklissi figures and regrettably the evidence from elsewhere is far too vague to shed any light on this matter.

The Apron

A familiar feature of early Imperial military sculpture is the 'apron' or sporran' worn by soldiers. Like the *Lorica Segmentata* the 'apron' was something the Roman soldier had gone without for centuries but which suddenly makes its appearance at the beginning of the Imperial period. The terms 'apron' or 'sporran' are of course modern, the correct Roman name is unknown and it may simply have been considered part of the belt.

Based on sculptural evidence, the apron rapidly developed from an overhanging surplus of a single belt into a number of separate studded strands finished with decorated terminals. These terminals are generally classed into two main categories; the tear drop shaped and the lunate. A third less popular type, the ivy leaf, is also known to exist. The majority of sculptures show four straps attached to an apron plate but a few soldiers have only one, Cottiedius Attianus from COHORS IX PRAETORIA has nine. Other apron features are the large rectangular plate at the top and the smaller plates above the hinged terminals. Plates, studs, and terminals could all be highly decorated.

There seems to be no obvious distinction between legionary and Auxiliary aprons which are equally elaborate if not more so. Nor is their any indication of rank in the number of straps worn. For example, Cordus, an ordinary soldier in XIV GEMINA has six straps while Cn. Musius an *Aquilifer* in the same Legion has only four. By the end of the First century AD, the apron was beginning to diminish in size and by the Third century it had ceased to be a feature of military equipment. So what had been its exact function?

The apron is generally described as being a form of protection for the lower stomach and private parts. Aprons, probably of leather straps, although without the metal studs, can be seen on sculptures of gladiators, one of the few forms of defence worn. An any re-enactor will tell you, however, the apron in fact offers very little protection, indeed it can be something of a nuisance and it is not unknown for the terminals to scratch the wearer's legs. As mentioned before most Roman armour developed to protect the soldier from slashing blows to the head and shoulders, not to the lower stomach. Additionally any modification to take into consideration Germanic stabbing weapons, were again concentrated on the upper body. An apron would not provide protection against either stabs or slashing cuts.

One interesting phenomenon which is discovered by anyone who has worn the longer mail shirt and

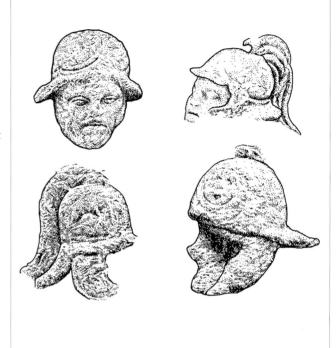

First Century AD helmets on Gallic reliefs.

then converts to plate armour is the naked feeling below the waist. A heavily studded apron can therefore offer an element of psychological protection, in addition the slightest movement on the part of the individual creates a degree of noise, an effect that must have been greatly multiplied when a whole army was on the move. This must have been highly intimidating to any enemy force as well as providing a sense of safety in numbers to the Roman soldier.

A further point must also be considered. The belt was one of the status symbols of the soldier marking him out from the ordinary citizens, it would seem the Auxiliaries especially were keen to emphasise this. Off duty and out of armour the soldier in his deliberately shortened tunic and decorated belts and apron would be instantly recognisable. One can easily imagine an individual soldier even if separated from his unit strutting through town with the apron jingling like the spurs of a western gunslinger.

Legionary Helmets

For centuries the Roman legionary was equipped with a simple bronze helmet known today by the term *Montefortino*, after an area of Northern Italy where

A reconstruction of an Augustan helmet found in Nijmegan probably the earliest in the Imperial Gallic series.

(above) Idria.

Opposite.

Top left.

Reconstruction of a bronze Montefortino helmet, late First century BC/early First century AD.

Top right.

A reconstructed helmet of Coolus type found at Drusenheim, this helmet is notable for its enlarged neck guard. It is also fitted with side plume tubes.

Bottom.

Reconstructed Imperial Gallic helmets from: (left) Kupa; (right) Mainz.

large numbers of this helmet were found. Originally displaying high standards of workmanship and elaborate detailing, these helmets declined in quality rapidly after the military reforms of the General Marius around 100 BC. Presumably this was because the *Montefortino* became the mass produced standard helmet of the Roman Army. The *Montefortino* also largely replaced other current types such as the *Attic* and *Corinthian* helmets based on helmets of Greek descent. Nevertheless both these types remained fashionable in Roman art and may well have been retained in use by senior officers.

At first the *Montefortino* was made from a hemispherical bowl beaten into shape, but as methods became cruder the majority were manufactured by spinning techniques. At the back of the helmet there was a very small peak at eye level and large cheek pieces which also covered the ears. Overall it provided good protection to the head from the long slashing swords wielded by the Celts. If it had a weakness it would be at the upper front of the helmet where heavy blows could be brought down uninterrupted. This was perhaps a problem exacerbated by declining standards of production. A crest knob was fitted at the helmet's apex which in earlier times had purple and black feathers inserted. By the end of the First century BC, these seem to have been replaced by a horse hair crest of either black or red.

Montefortino helmets owed their origins to Celtic examples and would finally evolve into a design almost identical to the *Coolus* type, another helmet of Celtic origin. Both these helmets are sometimes termed the 'Jockey' type because they resemble the modern racing cap worn by Jockeys, although with the peak reversed. Indeed it is a common fault by unsuspecting members

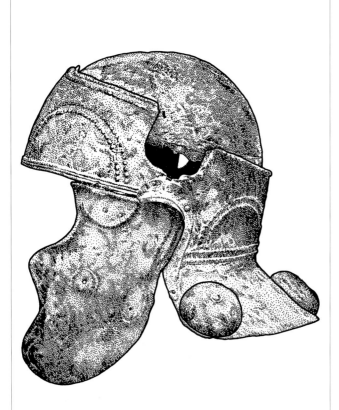

Top left.
Iron cavalry helmet with bronze covering from Ely dating to the First century AD.

Top right.
Early Second century AD bronze helmet probably for cavalry, now in Zagreb Museum.

Bottom.
Bronze helmet from Amerongen dating to the Second century AD.

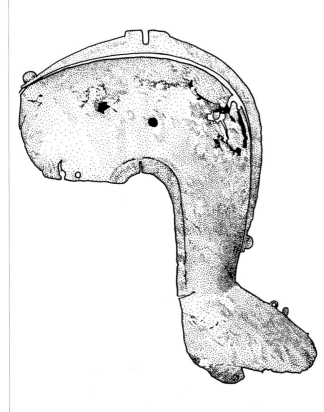

of the public to pick up reconstructed examples of these helmets and place them on their heads peak forward.

The first helmets of *Coolus* type originally lacked a crest knob being nothing more than a bowl shape with a small projecting peak at the rear. At some point in the First century BC the Romans altered the basic design of this helmet by the addition of a reinforcing peak at approximately eye-brow level. Sometime later further amendments included the lengthening of the rear peak and the added feature of a crest knob. In its most extreme form the rear peak also provided a measure of protection to the shoulders. Connolly suggested that the neck guard at eye level enabled the

Roman infantryman to fight in a crouched position against his Celtic adversary. Support for this theory comes from the fact that when the Romans first introduced designs based on other Celtic helmets they raised the neck guard from shoulder to eye level.

The use of crests seemed to be more important to the Romans rather than the Celts. The simplified design of the *Coolus* helmets was 'Romanised' by the otherwise superfluous crest knob. A further addition on later *Coolus* and *Montefortino* helmets were small hollow tubes on either side of the helmet. It is immediately evident that the otherwise plain appearance of these helmets can be greatly enhanced by the use of feathers in these tubes. One attractive

Above left.
Reconstruction of the Ely cavalry helmet.

Above right.
Rear view of reconstructed helmet from Weiler.

Below left.
Bronze cavalry helmet, First century AD found at Newstead. This is basically just the bowl of the helmet, lacking all its former fittings.

Below right.
Detail of a cavalryman on the Arch of Orange showing a *Coolus* type helmet.

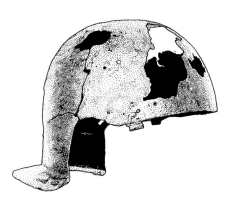

Reconstruction of an Imperial Gallic helmet found in an Amphitheatre at Besançon and dating to the latter part of the First century AD.

Reconstruction of a late First century AD Imperial Gallic helmet from Augsburg, showing a horsehair crest.

theory was recently proposed by Bishop in connection with these plume tubes and the possible identification of Caesar's LEGIO V ALAUDAE known as 'The Larks'. Bishop postulated that the feathers placed on these tubes emulated the appearance of the shore lark and was evidently a form of unit insignia easily distinguishable on the battlefield. Whether or not LEGIO V ALAUDAE continued this practice into Imperial times is uncertain, however plume tubes are still found on a number of helmets well into the First century AD.

There were various other methods of attaching crests including the drilling of a hole through the crest knob and fixing the crest by means of a pin. Alternatively the crest knob had a slot and the crest pin was further secured by its own retaining pin. It appears another procedure was by means of a small crest box. On some later helmets these crest boxes could be fastened to the front and rear of the helmet. It is not known for certain if these crest boxes and their later equivalents were of wood or metal. In either case they would be difficult to identify in an

archaeological context which would explain their apparent absence.

The wars of Caesar and Augustus in Gaul and Germany brought about a revolution in Roman helmet design. Although the *Coolus* type had initially been a cheaper alternative to the *Montefortino* it was already being superseded by yet other Celtic inspired designs. Two helmet variants in particular were adopted and adapted by the Roman army perhaps as early as the third quarter of the First century BC. These were the *Agen* and *Port* helmets which date to the middle of the First century BC. Many of the characteristics of these helmets, including their use of iron instead of bronze, distinctive cheek pieces, embossed eye brows and ribbing at the rear of the helmet all became trademarks of early Imperial Roman helmets.

The introduction of these helmets would have partially been a direct result of the influx of Celtic auxiliaries into the army, but perhaps more importantly the acquisition of large numbers of craftsmen as a consequence of the conquest of Gaul. Robinson identified two series of helmets in his

Rear view of a reconstructed iron Imperial Gallic helmet. This view shows the bronze carrying handle that became a feature of later versions of these helmets and the fitting on he top of the bowl for the crest attachment.

Reconstruction of a Third century iron helmet from Heddernheim. Helmets of this type were previously believed to be cavalry helmets because of the enclosed ears. However similar style helmets also appear on infantry tombstones.

classification of Roman Imperial helmets which he termed 'Imperial Gallic' and 'Imperial Italic', a typology which is largely followed in this book. It should be pointed out, however, that continental scholars favour a different scheme based on that of site nomenclature.

A feature of early helmets in the 'Gallic' and 'Italic' series are the cut outs for the ears. One helmet from Eich in Germany actually seems to have been a converted helmet perhaps formally belonging to a Celtic warrior. In its modified form cut outs for the ears were included. Ear cut outs were soon fitted with ear guards. It is noticeable that the ears of most modern re-enactors will fit comfortably inside the helmet so the addition of ear guards would seem to be somewhat superfluous. Late Republican and early Imperial portraits seem to imply that projecting ears were a common trait and this phenomenon can still be found amongst the inhabitants of the Naples district to this day. Russell Robinson too commented on the possibility that it was maybe this physical feature

which accounted for the large ear guards to be found on the 'Gallic' and 'Italic' helmets.

The majority of Imperial 'Gallic' helmets were made from iron bowls. They retained the embossed eye brows from the Celtic helmets, a feature possibly stylised on Roman sculpture as a pair of dolphins unless it was actually meant to indicate the origin of a Legion from the Marines. The bowl itself was trimmed with brass piping and decorated with brass bosses occasionally fitted with coloured enamel. Cheek pieces unlike those which survive on both *Montefortino* and *Coolus* helmets had rounded cut outs at eye and mouth level and are mostly decorated with a number of brass bosses. These too could be fitted with enamel. In addition the lower boss on the cheek-pieces was used to secure the chin tie rings on the inside.

On modern reconstructions, a leather thong is tied under the chin, passing through these rings behind the ears to a single ring riveted on the underside of the neck-guard. This makes any Roman helmet virtually

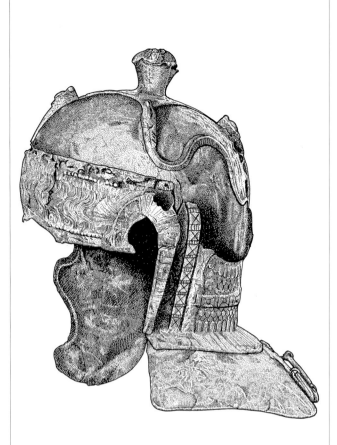

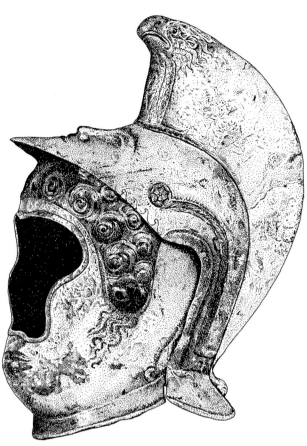

Iron and bronze cavalry helmet, late Second/early Third century, found at Heddernheim, the bronze decoration takes the form of Serpents and engraved scaling.

Bronze helmet which has been tinned all over. This helmet dates to the late Second century to early Third century. Found at Heddernheim it is usually described as a cavalry 'sports' helmet.

impossible to remove without the owner's consent. One other modified helmet of 'Gallic' type was recently found in Nijmegen, Holland. It seems though that many of the 'Gallic' features had been deliberately removed. Even more surprising were the trace of an animal skin cover with feathers attached which was found still adhering to the bowl. It has been suggested in view of the unusual nature of this particular helmet that it was therefore worn by a Germanic soldier serving in the Auxilia rather than by a legionary. But this is not the only evidence for there being some sort of protective cover worn over the helmet. At the siege of Dyrrachium during the Civil War between the forces of Caesar and Pompey, Pompey's soldiers were instructed to wear wickerwork fitted to their helmets. This defence constructed from osiers was a counter measure against stones hurled by the Caesarean defenders. A reminder that even in Roman times, under enlightened commanders soldiers were allowed to modify their equipment to suit battlefield conditions.

Furthermore, the practice of wearing animal skins over the helmets, normally employed by standard bearers may, according to Trajan's Column, have been more widespread. More than one soldier is shown with an animal pelt over his helmet. The type of shield carried by these soldiers is the normal infantry Auxiliary shield, nor did they carry standards but were originally holding ordinary spears, now lost. Of course this representation may have been a complete mistake on the part of the Column's sculptors, many other errors have been attributed to them, but the eccentricities of many Roman Emperors must be borne in mind in any study of the Roman army. Apart from their mail shirts, these figures are no more different than the class of Republican soldier known as a *Veles*, used as light infantry.

None of the 'Gallic' or 'Italic' type helmets were fitted with the knob form of crest holders instead a new different method of attaching the crest appeared, taking the form of a forked crest box holder which was either slotted of twisted into a plate on top of the helmet.

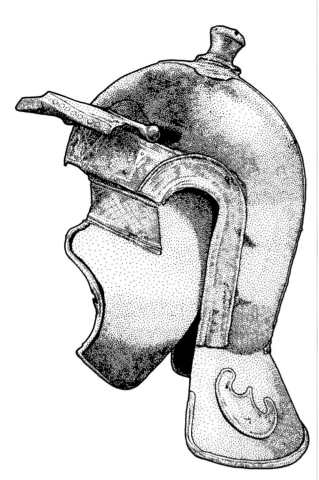

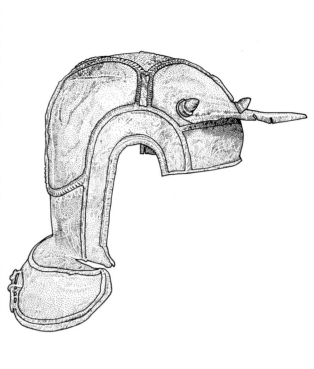

Third century iron cavalry helmet from Nijmegen.

Bronze cavalry helmet from Bodengraven, late Second to early Third century AD.

Caesar's account of the battle against the Nervii tribe in Gaul describes how his troops when caught by a surprise attack had no time to fix 'insignia' upon their helmets usually taken to mean crests, thereby implying that crests were normally worn in battle. Early Imperial sculpture suggests crests were worn in battle, however it is not certain how long this practice persisted into the First century AD.

By the time of the Emperor Trajan some helmets were fitted with reinforcing bars across the brow, making the wearing of a crest impossible. A situation confirmed by both Trajan's Column and the Adamklissi Tropaeum. The 'Italic' type helmets are of an inferior quality to their 'Gallic' contemporaries although they follow the same basic design, Robinson believed they were the products of Italian workshops. To support this he pointed out the number of elements of these helmets such as the archaic method of crest attachment which could even be found in Greek 'Attic' Helmets.

Soon after the adoption of both 'Gallic' and 'Italic' helmets the decision was made to lengthen the depth and angle of the rear neck guard. This was quite a departure from the previous eye level neck guards

which had been a consistent feature of Roman helmets for centuries. Although the Romans had encountered the Germanic tribes during Republican times it was only during the last years of the First century BC that the first of many long drawn out wars and campaigns against the Germans took place. The German tribes commonly used a short stabbing spear and Connolly believed it was as a result of these weapons that the Romans revised their fighting techniques. In his opinion the Romans adopted a more upright posture when engaged against the enemy. Helmet design was therefore effected by this change as greater protection was required to the neck and shoulders than before. However this may initially only have been a local response to local conditions because helmets retaining the eye level neck guards were not phased out entirely and are still found at a later date on the Danubian frontier. Here the Romans faced the Dacians who still largely used long slashing weapons. The development of extra protection for the head did continue, until by the Third century AD the head was almost totally encased. Additionally the crossed reinforcing bars were strengthened and raised higher from the bowl.

74 *Armour and Helmets*

These cross reinforcing bars have led to the modern nickname of the 'Hot cross bun' type being applied to these helmets.

It is a necessary requirement that a helmet needs a lining, supplemented by extra padding to suit the individual, if not simple forms of cloth perhaps even a type of cap. It is almost certain that leather, linen or woollen materials were used one way or another. Only in extreme conditions does any trace of a lining survive. And yet from time to time this occurs, indeed confirming that leather was used, often fixed by animal glues. This definitely applies to the insides of the cheek pieces but it is not so clear whether a lining was glued into the entire helmet. Robinson suggested that linings may have been similar to those in use on later medieval helmets. In that instance segments of material were joined up together at the pointed end by an adjustable lace, a method which survived into modern times.

The late Roman historian Vegetius describes how soldiers in earlier Roman times wore a cap even during off duty hours to accustom themselves to the weight of the helmet. Art from the later Empire confirms the existence of two types of cap used by military personnel. The most common form is a round 'pill-box' type probably of felt or wool known as a *Pileus Pannonicus*. Its use was widespread, popular with all ranks from the humblest soldier to the Emperor. Another was the elaborate *Phrygian* cap with extended ear flaps and a pointed extension on the top. In appearance it is similar to the 'red cap' of liberty familiar from French history or less glamorously that of a garden gnome. Needless to say this type of headgear has little appeal to modern re-enactors.

Other forms of headgear were doubtless used by off-duty soldiers, although there is very little evidence at all for hats of any kind in the Roman world. One rare depiction shows what is most likely a straw hat worn by a fisherman on a mosaic in Sousse Museum. Another hat which would appear to be of straw can be seen in both *The story of Marsyas* and *Odysseus in the land of the Laestrygonians*, both frescoes from Rome and Pompeii, it has a small bowl and a wide brim.

There are two final possibilities for what might possibly be worn beneath Roman helmets. Next to the soldiers with the animal skin head-dress on Trajan's Column are other figures wearing some sort of head protector. Its shape is similar to those worn today by Rugby players or cyclists with a rib like structure. As

Opposite.
Reconstructed cavalry in 'sports' equipment in front of the 'Heidentor' at Carnuntum.

Cavalry helmet of the early First century AD based on an iron helmet found in a grave at Weiler.

well as this reference, often doubted for its complete accuracy, this type of headgear is also shown on another stone relief. Finally on a fresco from Pompeii featuring the hero Aeneas being treated for a wound, a group of soldiers can also be seen in the background. One of them is wearing a white cap, instead of a helmet, which is tied underneath his chin. This may be the type of cap referred to by an account of the soldier and historian Ammianus Marcellinus. Marcellinus describes how a cap from inside a helmet was used as a means of obtaining water by lowering it into a well tied to strips of fabric. From this account at least we can assume it was either waterproof or could retain water.

Auxiliary Infantry Helmets

The study of helmets belonging to the Auxiliary infantry has been somewhat handicapped by Robinson's assertion that they were generally inferior in quality to those of the legionaries. His own study presented only two examples from the First century. These were a simple bronze spun helmet from Fluren and a well preserved helmet found in the Rhine at

Second century face mask from a cavalry sports helmet found at Hebron with an iron italic infantry helmet.

A female cavalry sports face mask probably representing an Amazon, found amongst a hoard of material discovered at Straubing.

Mainz also in Germany. This latter version was, as Robinson pointed out, nothing more than a contemporary Legionary helmet devoid of all its fittings.

This disparity in numbers between legionary and Auxiliary helmets is clearly a serious imbalance if, as we are led to believe, there were as many Auxiliary troops as legionaries. If the criteria that Auxiliary helmets were simplified versions of legionary ones this could be extended to include many versions of the later bronze *Monterfortino* and *Coolus* designs. It would seem this is borne out by a soldier on the Mainz Column base, usually regarded as an Auxiliary by the fact that he is equipped with a flat oval shield. He is wearing a helmet that could be either of these two variants. One suggestion has been that the Auxilia were supplied with obsolete legionary helmets, although this would conflict with another widely held belief that equipment was retained as long as it was serviceable.

Some First century helmets can be positively identified as legionary because they are inscribed with their owners' names. These are invariably proof of

Roman citizenship, therefore legionary, but as service in the Auxilia became increasingly attractive to Roman citizens, as the century wore on this situation becomes more confused. Evidence from grave stelae is of little value as without exception auxiliary tombstones show the deceased minus his helmet, but here too the evidence would suggest that overall, Auxiliary equipment was not to dissimilar to that worn by the legionaries.

From the time of Trajan this situation changes somewhat as a number of helmets of various types are depicted on reliefs of Auxiliary soldiers. Firstly a version very similar to the Celtic *Agen* type with a reinforcing brow guard that completely encircles the helmet. Both infantry and cavalrymen wear this helmet, but this could possibly have been a device on the part of the sculptors to emphasise the ethnic nature of the Imperial forces to a Roman audience. Secondly, a helmet of conical design which on Trajan's column is used exclusively by archers. Conical helmet design was popular amongst the Parthians and Persians throughout the Roman period, therefore an

Top.

Silvered bronze dragon head from a Sarmatian style standard. A pole would have been attached beneath and a tube of coloured material fixed behind. When air passed through the open mouth it caused the tube to writhe and hiss.

Top right.

Cavalry 'sports' helmet found at Ribchester now in the British Museum. It probably dates to the later First century AD.

© British Museum.

Bottom right.

Tombstone of Aurelius Lucius, a cavalrymen from Chester, his helmet would appear to have both crest and plumes.

© Grosvenor Museum, Chester.

Eastern origin for these helmets has always been put forward. A point reinforced by the long flowing robes worn by these archers.

Again it has been argued that this could be a means of highlighting the exotic nature of the Auxiliary forces to an impressionable public in the Capitol. A number of archers' tombstones do exist and on these provincial monuments they appear no differently from other auxiliary troops. One tombstone in particular from Housesteads on Hadrian's Wall gives no indication of the long tunic being worn, even though the Syrian origin of this soldier is beyond doubt, he may however wear a conical helmet and many reconstructions in the past have shown this, but the monument is badly worn and this is far from clear. And yet conical helmets do exist, a particular fine example is now in Zagreb museum. In overall appearance it has been compared to one on a tombstone of a Sarmatian cavalry standard bearer in the Grosvenor Museum, Chester, and it is quite possible that conical helmets belonged to Sarmatian mounted units rather than to infantry archers. Further support comes from a 'T' inscription on a conical helmet from Intercissa,

Two re-enactors demonstrate the basic tactics of the *Hyppika Gymnasia*, one man acts as a target while the other throws dummy javelins at him.

the possibility being that 'T' is an abbreviated form of *Turma*, the cavalry equivalent of an infantry Century.

Further Trajanic sculptures show Auxiliaries wearing conventional 'Attic' helmets but conceivably an actual auxiliary helmet from this period may survive in the Museo Archaeologico in Florence. It is a bronze skull piece from a badly damaged helmet but its crossed reinforces correspond to helmets of the late

Opposite.

Top.

Based on a 'sports' helmet discovered with the Straubing hoard, this reconstruction was produced for the Archaeological Park Carnuntum. The rear view shows that embossed hair designs were still popular in the Third century AD and rings for attaching plumes.

Bottom.

Decorative cavalry 'sports' armour and trappings based on complete examples found in a hoard discovered at Straubing dating to the Third century AD. Reconstructions made for the Archaeological Park Carnuntum.

Second and early Third centuries. Monumental sculpture of the late Second century, such as the columns of Marcus Aurelius and Antonine Sarcophagi, as well as illustrating traditional classical styles feature another less familiar contender for an auxiliary helmet. This takes the form of a helmet which echoes the brimmed helmet of Trajan's Column but has a bowl that is brought forward from the apex in a style

In cavalry sports according to Arrian, a 'Scythian' dragon standard was used like this reconstruction made for the Archaeological Park at Carnuntum. These standards were later adopted into the Roman army.

resembling the *Phrygian* cap, a popular garment in Greek times and comparable to helmets which were common in the Macedonian army of Alexander the Great. Again there is no archaeological evidence for such a design so it must be concluded that the sculptors were not attempting to portray any existing battle helmet. The same could be said for the examples of sculptured helmets with a large ring crest, although the fact that both auxiliaries and legionaries wear these helmets is an interesting one.

Auxiliary Cavalry Helmets

Whereas the helmets of Auxiliary infantry are poorly recorded, those of Auxiliary cavalry by comparison are well represented. In all probability this reflected their superior pay and status, although in the past this point has not always been recognised. At the beginning of the reign of Augustus the majority of the Gallic and German auxiliaries would no doubt have supplied their own equipment including helmets if they owned any. In addition any distinctions between infantry and cavalry helmets which might have existed may have been forgotten in the confusion of the Civil Wars.

On the Arch at Orange, built to commemorate the suppression of a Gallic rebellion in AD21, the cavalrymen appear to wear a *Coolus* type helmet although these could well be legionary cavalrymen. In which case it would be understandable for them to be equipped with a ready supply of cheaply available helmets. 'Jockey' type helmets are far from satisfactory for cavalrymen as they don't provide sufficient protection for the nape of the neck. In addition the large neck guard could prove disastrous to any rider unfortunate to be knocked off his horse.

Examples of a highly distinctive class of helmets appear in some detail on a number of surviving Cavalry grave stelae like that of Romanius Capito from Mainz. Although generally tombstones are not always reliable, in this particular instance it is verified by an increasing amount of archaeological evidence.

These helmets are easily distinguished by their bowls which were made of iron and then covered with thin copper alloy. In turn this was embossed to look like human hair. A number of examples of this curious fashion have now come to light. Helmets from Nijmegen, although of the class of helmets termed cavalry 'Parade' helmets, are covered with a curious bonnet of human or animal hair which may have proceeded the use of embossing on these and battle helmets. A recently discovered Cavalry helmet from Xanten was also covered with a similar 'hair net'.

Although many Roman sculptures depict some form of decoration on helmet cheek pieces usually in the manner of mythological symbols, this is not always backed up by archaeological finds. Cavalry cheek pieces are sometimes highly decorated with mythological scenes, individual figures, or in the case of a piece from Xanten a continuation of the embossed hair decoration. Unlike infantry cheek pieces those on cavalry helmets also provided protection for the ear as well. Hearing is bad enough in an infantry helmet so the difficulty of hearing anything in a cavalry helmet, particularly above the noise produced by a scale shirt, can well be imagined. Cavalry helmets were now invariably fitted with either a smaller neck guard or a deeply angled one. One example of the latter type was an iron helmet found in Ely, Cambridgeshire. The neck guard was fitted with large bronze bosses and another was attached to the front of the bronze brow.

Whereas the distinctive features of First century cavalry helmets is in marked contrast to the contemporary infantry helmets, by the end of the Second century the picture once again becomes confused. Helmets with all the characteristics of cavalry helmets are also represented on infantry grave stelae. This has therefore led some historians to re-assess the available evidence and arrive at a new conclusion. Instead of a clear distinction between infantry and cavalry helmets it is now believed many troop types wore an equivalent design which gave greater protection to the head and face leaving only a 'T' shaped opening at the front for the eyes and mouth. Helmets with their angled peaks and crossed reinforces were obviously a counter measure against the fighting techniques of mainly Germanic opponents. In turn this has also led to something of a reassessment of the large body of so called 'Sports' helmets which come from the Third century. Many of these helmets are so labelled simply on account of their ostentatious decoration.

Many First century battle helmets could equally be described as elaborate, those with embossed hair designs for example. A tinned brass helmet with embossed decoration and eagle crest from the Thielenhofen is another of later date. This example is particularly instructive because it apparently belonged to a humble cavalry trooper in COHORS III BRACARAUGUSTANORUM EQUITATAE, usually regarded as one of the most inferior type of units in the Roman army. Conceivably therefore some of the 'sports' helmets may well have been battle equipment. Two almost identical helmets from Syria may illustrate this. One was fitted with a face mask, the other had the 'T' shaped face opening. The suggestion now is that it is these latter helmets should be considered as battle helmets.

Sports Helmets and Equipment

The events known as the *Hippika Gymnasia*, where cavalrymen competed in teams have been described as the Roman equivalent of the medieval tournament or as a martial display designed to impress the 'natives'. No doubt they fulfilled both these functions as well as providing an additional opportunity for practising battlefield skills and tactics. The troopers wore highly decorated and colourful equipment for these occasions although some of the equipment so described may well have been normal battle gear. The best source for these displays comes from the Second century AD historian and soldier Arrian and from him we hear of brightly coloured tunics in scarlet, red or blue and hyacinth. The cavalrymen too wore tight fitting trousers beneath their tunics which may also have been as equally decorated.

According to Arrian, after forming a mounted *Testudo*, the riders divided into two teams, one team hurling wooden javelins at the other riders who later on took their own turn to throw. After this all the riders gave demonstrations in javelin throwing. The winner being the rider who threw both the most and over the greatest distance. For protection the riders wore helmets fitted with face masks, which come in both male and female designs, implying the contestants re-enacted the combat between Greeks and Amazons during the Trojan War. The masks were either fitted by means of a hinge or a hook on the underside of the helmet bowl. Another method included straps attached to the masks buckled behind the helmet. Arrian mentions yellow plumes fitted to the helmets, while the mask, like the helmet bowl, was decorated with embossed designs. The representation of wavy hair on many First Century cavalry helmets was used on sports helmets as well. Other helmet designs have prominent projecting peaks which may also have been based on regular issue helmets. Helmet peaks may be detected on the tombstones of standard bearers, both infantry and cavalry. Greaves could have been worn but Arrian does not record this, although as this is a personal observation there is plenty of scope for regional variations or developments over time.

The elaborate oval shields from Dura Europos have often been put forward as 'parade' or 'sports' type shields. Arrian mentions oblong shields, probably closer to the Doncaster type. But again this possibility need not be ruled out. Arrian does state that they were lighter than battle shields, which does in that instance seem to rule out Dura style shields. The horses too would require a degree of protection. This could have been similar to the horse armour from Dura Europos, while both metal and leather chamfrons and eye guards are known from archaeological finds. Some of this equipment could be for sports but equally would be appropriate for use in battle.

The standards that Arrian describes in use during the displays are very like those used by the Sarmatians on Trajan's Column. These are the wind sock standards where the head is fashioned in to the form of a serpent. Air passes through the open mouth of the serpent and fills out the tail behind. The tail itself is constructed from a patchwork of differently coloured dyed cloth. Arrian was particularly impressed by the hissing sound they made as the riders moved about.

Military Clothing

Tunics and Cloaks

In 1850, two brothers from Kirby Malzeard, near Ripon, North Yorkshire were digging for peat on nearby Grewelthorpe Moor. As so often happens in the history of archaeology, the right discovery was made at the wrong time. A well preserved male body was uncovered, his clothing too had miraculously survived and even traces of their original colours were still visible. Sadly by the time a local policeman arrived both body and clothing had almost been completely destroyed. Fortunately the policeman did manage to save a few fragments of the textiles and the sandals, parts of these are still on display in the Yorkshire Museum. The original description of the clothes recorded a greenish toga, a tunic with some scarlet material and stockings of yellow cloth, all consistent with the Roman period. Over the years some doubts were expressed about these remains, but a recent reassessment concluded the remains were almost certainly Roman in origin. The remains of the hobnailed shoe in particular were undoubtedly Roman. One modern commentator suggested the body had been that of a Roman soldier but without proper investigation it would be impossible to say. Hobnailed shoes could equally be civilian and no associated military finds were recorded with the body.

As in many aspects of archaeology it is from such tantalising glimpses of the past that most of our current knowledge is based. This is no more applicable than in the study of ancient textiles where the evidence is fragmentary. By comparisons with other clues from contemporary civilian fashions portrayed in art, tombstones and sculptures, literary accounts and surviving textiles, it is just about possible to reconstruct the type of tunic worn by Roman soldiers.

In all likelihood these tunics would have been of either linen or wool following a very basic pattern. This would have been simply two pieces of material roughly 1m square sewn together at the sides but leaving openings for the head and arms. 'Tea bag' shaped is an apt description. This was not the fashion amongst the peoples of Northern Europe and some Celtic and Germanic auxiliaries may well have retained their long sleeved tunics. The tombstone of the cavalryman Flavius Bassus from Cologne shows this with the addition of sleeve cuffs turned back. This is identical to the tunic worn by the Celtic warrior in Avignon Museum, also perhaps a cavalryman. There appears to have been other variations on the overall design including one similar to a modern 'T'-shirt and another which enabled the right shoulder to be bared. This allowed the wearer to swing his right arm freely, an action that would be required when wielding a pickaxe. This latter feature is commonly shown when illustrating scenes of manual activity such as those carried out by farm labourers in the fields. Not surprisingly on Trajan's Column in the one scene which shows soldier cutting down trees and moving earth, they too wear this type of tunic.

Under normal circumstances this tunic appears to have been gathered together in a bunched knot at the back of the neck, probably tied by a leather thong. An identical arrangement can still be observed in use by the nomads of Mauretania. These knots at the back can be seen on Trajan's Column but are also paralleled elsewhere such as on the Chatsworth relief and the Belvedere Sacophagus both depicting soldiers. Whether this type of tunic was widely worn throughout the army or just by soldiers expected to carry out engineering works, the equivalent of pioneers, it is impossible to say. Whereas there are benefits to this type of tunic, a knot at the back of the neck can be an added discomfort underneath armour. From the beginning of the Third century AD onwards sleeved tunics, perhaps as a result of increasing Germanic influence, were worn by all ranks.

Of one thing, however, we are certain, it was undoubtedly the military fashion to wear the tunic belted. The tunic would normally reach to the mid-calf but when belted would be hitched up above the

Top left and right.

Two views of a reconstructed tunic. The right side will open to allow freedom of movement during manual work. For normal wear it can be tied up at the back with a leather thong.

knees. This was obviously seen as a soldier's distinguishing characteristic and may help to explain the attention that was placed on decorating the belt. A minor military punishment emphasising this point was the removal of the offenders belt who was then forced to stand in the camp in his un-girthed tunic, stripped of his soldier's dignity! On many grave stelae of the First century and in particular those of the Auxilia, it appears that the tunic was somehow pulled up at the sides as well, perhaps tucked under the belt. This has the result of curving the bottom edge of the tunic as well as creating numerous folds. It is nevertheless difficult to recreate this appearance satisfactorily with a thick woollen tunic, this leads to the possibility that a second 'undress' tunic of lighter material, feasibly of fine wool or linen, was worn perhaps as the soldier's off duty uniform or on a special parades.

The existence of at least a second tunic may help to solve one current perplexing problem, that of the colour of the Roman military tunic. This problem has undoubtedly arisen as a direct result of the existence of

re-enactment groups with their need to present an accurate picture of military life. Apart from a few exceptions previously, little attention had been paid to the study of textiles, but modern scientific research now extends beyond the simple examination of artefacts attempting to place everything in its overall context. There is plenty of evidence to suggest the military purchased, compulsory or otherwise, material or ready-made tunics from amongst the local population. These tunics or cloaks could then be delivered to the nearest garrison as confirmed by a papyrus receipt from Egypt. This records the delivery of nineteen tunics and five white cloaks which were to be sent to the army in Judaea. A pay receipt belonging to a Roman Soldier from Masada also records linen and white tunics as well as an 'overall' cloak.

White woollens or linens would obviously be materials which had been left in their natural un-dyed state. Amongst the textiles from Masada, the linen finds, with one exception, had been left un-dyed whilst approximately half the woollen textiles had been dyed. Some of the Masada textiles were dyed red which survived in a variety of shades, ranging from a deep red to salmon pink. In the case of Masada, as indeed on many other Roman sites, the majority probably belonged to the Jewish defenders and civilians

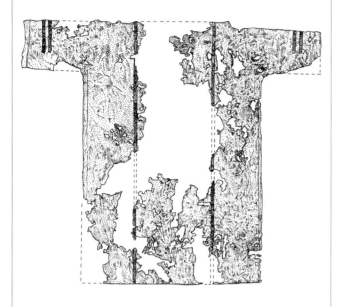

Restored tunic based on a near complete example found at Dura Europos. It would be hard to say if it was definitely a military tunic but the shape would not be too different.

associated with the famous siege. It is very likely most of the textiles, with Gamma patterns known from Jewish sources, or the more colourful examples came from women's garments.

Portrait paintings from Roman Egypt gives a good impression of the range of colours worn in Roman times, and these have close parallels with the finds from Masada. Bright red or scarlet does not appear to have been worn by women who are generally pictured in dark blue, purple, dark red and pink garments. Some of these Egyptian portraits have been described as soldiers, an identification based on their use of studded red belts, unfortunately none of these portraits are full length which would confirm this. These particular examples show males in white tunics with dark blue cloaks. An amazing letter from a soldier recruited in Egypt does actually mention how he commissioned a portrait of himself as a record for his family. It would of course be fairly natural for a soldier to be depicted in an off duty uniform of tunic, cloak and belt, if the

Leggings on a relief from Nijmegen.

Egyptian pictures are indeed soldiers this would confirm the wearing of a white tunic on occasions.

The only detailed study of tunics and cloaks was carried out by Fuentes, although he himself did admit it was not exhaustive. His study was based on mosaics, wall paintings and literary sources covering the period from the Third century BC. to about 300 AD. Fuentes proposed that legionaries wore white tunics at all times. To distinguish them in battle he suggested Centurions, including those in command of ships, wore red tunics and senior officers like their men wore white tunics possibly of finer material. Cloaks were almost without exception a yellow brown colour, not unlike those still worn in parts of North Africa, which may well be descended from Roman originals. In addition Fuentes believed Centurions were further distinguished by red cloaks and helmet crests. But contrary to this the historian Vegetius only mentions a crest as the Centurions' distinguishing characteristic; he does not refer to any colour. Senior officers may well have worn white cloaks such as those described on the Egyptian papyri.

Another attractive theory was the possibility that Naval personnel wore a light blue tunic. A late Fourth century literary account actually refer to ships, sails and sailors' tunics being the same colour as the sea, an early example of camouflage. Fuentes too has to admit

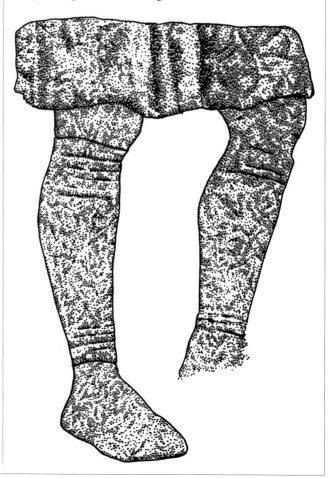

that in his scheme, in the event of special festivities such as religious or triumphal parades even the Centurions were obliged to wear white. During the triumphal entry of the Emperor Vitellius into Rome in AD. 69 both the Tribunes and Centurions are specifically described as wearing bleached white garments. Fuentes does not mention the Egyptian portraits. Their blue cloaks would conflict with the otherwise uniform suggestions of yellow brown as the accepted colour, although one soldier on a fresco from Castellum Dimidi seems to have a blue grey cloak.

Cheapness of materials was no doubt a consideration for the Romans as in countless other armies down the centuries. Tunics left there natural un-dyed colour would obviously fulfil this criteria. In similar circumstances the large Royal Armies of France and Austria also adopted white uniforms in the Seventeenth and Eighteenth centuries. It has often been stated that white tunics worn under armour or in action would easily get dirty. Somewhat ironically there was a movement by some French Revolutionary officers to return to the royal white uniform because they were easier to keep clean. Likewise the adoption

of red uniforms by the British had less than heroic reasons. Red dye was cheap. In Roman times a number of red dyes were available but madder *Rubia tinctorum* was perhaps the most commonly used. In Britain it is feasible that bed straw and even mushrooms were possible sources of red dye.

Bright colours like red are also dependent on the mordant used as well as the dye. Throughout the Mediterranean world, aluminium was one popular mordant but other materials such as wood ash, urine, sheep manure and club mosses could also serve this purpose. A number of the textiles recovered from the pre-Hadrianic Fort at Vindolanda near Hadrian's Wall were analysed for dyes. All of the textiles were sheep's wool and out of fifty fragments investigated, eight showed traces of being dyed. In all instances, madder red appeared to have been the dye used. The only other dye detected was what appeared to have been a purple stripe on an otherwise plain textile. In all likelihood this may have come from a tunic belonging to the commanding officer of the fort.

There exist a few other examples of red tunics in military usage. Catacomb paintings while obviously representing religious scenes from the Old and New Testament generally depicted characters in

Leg wrapping from Sogaards Mose, Denmark. This type of garment is identical to those depicted on Roman reliefs including one from Nijmegen.

A leg wrapping from Sogaards Mose unwrapped.

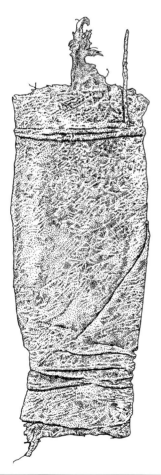

A military cloak of a type known as a *Sagum*.

Reconstruction of a First century AD undress uniform, based on both legionary and Auxiliary sculptured grave stelae, of the First century.

contemporary dress, the cavalrymen on the Dura Europos frescoes for example. Flavius Maximianus, a soldier in the Auxilia Palatina, is shown on the Via Maria catacomb paintings in Syracuse wearing a red tunic with dark red patches. Tunics of this style became popular in the later Fourth and Fifth centuries AD. The overall accuracy of this picture is heightened by the crested ridge helmet, complete with eye shaped ornaments, a remarkable parallel to an actual example from Intercissa in Hungary. In addition this soldier carries a spear and a white shield with a yellow design.. A recently discovered circular shield from Egypt also shows a military figure or god wearing a red cloak and tunic, holding a spear and shield. Another source of evidence are later medieval manuscript copies of Roman originals, one in particular now in the Bibliotheque Nationale, Paris shows a very detailed figure in a red tunic. Like the 'Via Maria' fresco it is the soldier's accessories which makes this picture interesting. These include the famous 'pill box' fur hat so familiar from many late Roman sculptures and the stockings that the soldier wears. These are both well documented details from Roman sculptures and mosaics.

Although the crested helmets of the Syracuse figures may indicate junior officer status the accoutrements that these soldiers carry seem to suggest otherwise, especially in the case of the manuscript figure there is no indication that any attempt to portray an officer was intended. In addition two soldiers in red tunics, one thrusting his lance into Christ at the crucifixion, another asleep at the Resurrection in an illuminated manuscript now in the Biblioteca Laurenziana, Florence, are also unlikely to be officers. It would not be to difficult to find a reason for the wearing of red tunics in the Roman army. Red was a popular colour in the Greek and especially Macedonian Army. Etruscan and Ptolemaic soldiers too are shown in red tunics as indeed are also some early Republican Romans. Red therefore would be perceived as a traditional military colour, indeed it is referred to as such on the list of personal belongings of the Emperor Claudius II while serving in Syria as a *Tribune* in the late Roman army.

Claudius owned a number of white tunics, one of which was partly of silk but significantly he also had two red 'military' tunics. The suggestion that a tribune would wear red again conflicts with the system suggested by Fuentes. One belief is that a sudden change to white in the Roman army took place due to the influx of recruits resulting from the reforms at the beginning of the First century BC, and the need to equip them cheaply. However this reason was not put forward by Fuentes who believed the Roman army always wore white. Some of the evidence above could suggest the later Imperial army wore red tunics and as this was as large, if not larger, than that of the earlier Empire this would have been a complete reversal of a former policy under comparable conditions. The use of a limited range of colours by the Roman army would seem to be evident and the possibility exists that soldiers of all ranks had more than one tunic, wearing perhaps one of a superior quality and perhaps different colour for parades and off duty wear.

Stockings, Socks and Leggings

The notion that socks or stockings were worn by soldiers was first brought to general attention by one of the earliest Vindolanda writing tablets, where a

Even this small detachment of reconstructed legionaries reveals the wide variety of helmets that were in contemporary use in the late First century AD.

soldier thanked a relative or friend for the gift of a pair of socks and underpants. Incidentally a child's sock was later found at this same site. But the existence of these simple garments are known from a number of other sources not least with the remains of bodies, like those from Grewelthorpe Moor. Socks were obviously a popular accessory in the Northern Provinces, although a painting from Egypt also shows a women wearing socks.

A closer study of the Cancellaria relief in Rome revealed the fact that one of the members of the Praetorian guard was wearing open toed and healed socks under his sandals. Many examples of Roman footwear had numerous cut outs in the leather and brightly coloured socks worn underneath would have looked quite attractive. Agricultural labourers and huntsmen both on foot and mounted are often depicted wearing knee high stockings or simple tubes of material, probably of wool, tied below the knee and above the ankle. Similar garments were discovered with the Danish bog bodies and are also frequently associated with reliefs of hunters, many of whom could well have been soldiers. Stockings would have provided a measure of protection against thorns and other similar hazards encountered in the country and it would not be to far fetched if soldiers added them to their uniform as required, a simple form of battlefield

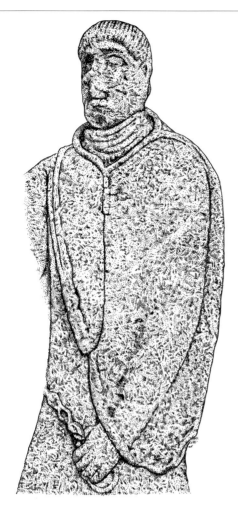

Detail of a figure from the Adamklissi Tropaeum showing the *Paenula* **style of cloak, its method of fastening and probably a long scarf beneath.**

Detail of a late Third century soldier from a fresco now largely destroyed at the Pharaonic Temple of Luxor which had been converted into a Roman fort. He carries a staff suggestive of rank and a fringed cloak.

modification that cannot be proved either way.

Two other examples may support this suggestion. On the tombstone of the Trainee Lanciarius Aurelius Mucianus from Apamea, Mucianus appears to have socks rolled down over the top of his boots. Additionally on the fresco of the Tribune from Dura Europos some of the foreground figures, including Tribune Julius Terentius, are either wearing boots up to mid calf which would be unusual, or alternatively ankle boots and socks. Whereas the wearing of socks under sandals provides a degree of comfort, this situation disappears when the sandals and socks get wet. However when the Roman army footwear changed from an open sandal to a more enclosed boot, socks may will have been worn as a matter of course.

Another piece of evidence for socks may well have been unrecognised for a long time. At about the same period as the army changed from sandal style boots to enclosed footwear, legionaries in particular are also seen apparently wearing breeches to just below the knee. It has always been assumed that these are breeches and that the legionaries had adopted the

fashion after contact with the Germans and Celts. However breeches do not appear to have been worn by either the Celts or Germans who seem to have favoured longer trousers, although presumably Celtic and German auxiliaries on Trajan's Column are represented in unusually short tunics and breeches.

On many of the sculptured examples available which depict legionary figures, in so called breeches, a line has simply been made across the leg below the knee. There is no attempt to depict any folds or other suggestion of material which is clearly evident on the breeches worn by Auxiliaries on Trajan's Column, leading to the conclusion that all these other breeches were fairly tight fitting. However instead of a garment being above this line, an alternative explanation could be that it is in fact a knee length sock that was originally intended. It has been mentioned before that sculptured monuments were rendered in colour and this sort of detail could well have been picked out in paint. Many other anomalies would have long been cleared up if the paint had survived into modern times.

A mosaic from Apamea actually shows a huntsmen wearing both breeches to just above the knee and leggings to just below the knee.

By the Fourth century, a different type of leg protection had appeared, this is seen on many African and middle Eastern hunting scenes such as on the great hunting mosaic from Piazza Armerina in Sicily, figures in the manuscripts from Paris and Florence mentioned earlier, and many depictions of Christ as the good shepherd. Although the details are not exactly clear it would seem strips of material were wrapped around the lower leg in a fashion reminiscent of puttees worn by First World War infantry. This later Roman fashion may well have been following a style that had been around much longer than at first supposed.

Cloaks

The ordinary soldiers of the Roman army of the early years in the Empire appear to have worn two particular styles of cloaks, the *Sagum* and the *Paenula*. Officers of the rank of Centurion and above on the other hand seems to have favoured a cloak called the *Paludamentum*. The *Sagum* like most Roman costume was very basic in design consisting simply of a rectangular piece of heavy woollen cloth. It was said by the Roman historian Varro to be of Gallic origin, however it is also identifiable amongst German and Spanish tribes.

Roman sculptures such as Trajan's Column show that by this date the *Sagum* and its slightly shorter derivative, the *Sagutum*, was the most popular form of cloak worn by troops. Trajan himself and some of his officers are wearing it, although it would be expected that their cloaks were of a finer weave. So common indeed was the *Sagum* amongst the military that it entered literature and became a byword for war. For this reason it was certainly banned for a time by the cultured Emperor Marcus Aurelius for being too militaristic. A number of cloaks on Trajan's Column are shown with fringed edges and this is confirmed by other examples both in sculpture and on wall paintings. Whether this was a sign of rank it is impossible to say with any certainty but it would seem to be associated with higher grade troops, *Beneficiarii* cavalrymen, standard bearers, and some officers such as Tribunes. One or two other examples show tassels at the bottom corners.

Where evidence for colour is available the majority suggests cloaks were left a natural yellow brown. Yellow brown cloaks are worn by both officers and men but it would be expected that officers would have cloaks made from superior material. Officers it seems may have had the choice of other colours such as red or white, while Egyptian portraits and one fresco suggest blue or blue grey as other possibilities. The *Sagum* was fastened over the right shoulder leaving a gap for the sword arm. A number of brooch fastenings are known, the most common being the simple 'C' shaped *Penannular* and 'P' shaped trumpet brooch. Both these types had many developments and were probably derived from native sources, despite their classical trappings.

An alternative to the *Sagum*, at least in the First century AD, was the cape-like *Paenula*. The *Paenul,a* judging from sculptural evidence alone, was probably oval in shape with a central hole for the soldier's head. It is sometimes described as having a hood attached and indeed hooded capes which just covered both head and shoulders, or reached almost to the ankles, are known from civilian contexts. It is not possible to say whether the *Paenula* used by the military had a hood or not, certainly while wearing a helmet it would not be necessary. According to the Roman historian Pliny, the *Paenula* neck opening meant the wearing of a large scarf was recommended. The bunching of a scarf around the neck may therefore have often been misinterpreted as a hood in the past.

The *Paenula* reached to the knees and was fastened up the front, not by brooches like the *Sagum*, but apparently by a combination of buttons and toggles like those on a modern duffle coat. This method of fastening is exceptionally clear on the tombstone of a soldier recovered from Camomile Street in London now on display at the museum of London. The slit up the front of the *Paenula* meant the two sides could be thrown back over the shoulders enabling the soldier to easily reach his sword and dagger. Occasionally the two 'tails' of material that are left at the front as a result of this manoeuvre even appear to have been decorated with an embroidered design.

The distinctive cloaks worn by Centurions, senior officers, and the Emperors, the *Paludamentum*, was worn more as a badge of office rather than as a practical garment. It would appear to have been rectangular like the *Sagum* but with the lower corners cut away. The *Paludamentum* was draped and fastened over the left shoulder and often partially wrapped around the left arm. Although some officers and guards are seen wearing yellow brown cloaks like those of their troops, Pliny also recorded that scarlet dye from the 'Coccum' was used for *Paludamentum*, while other sources refer to Generals wearing scarlet cloaks.

The Scarf

The wearing of a scarf around the neck is seen as

essential by modern re-enactors. A scarf provides a degree of comfort and protects the neck from the chaffing of all types of armour. Legionaries on Trajan's Column are certainly shown wearing a scarf under their *Lorica Segmentata* but surprisingly the auxiliaries wear theirs outside their mail shirts.

As our only source for the scarf is sculptural it is impossible to say what shape it was originally. A triangular shape is often used by modern re-enactors as this fits comfortably beneath the armour. However off duty soldiers may well have worn a simple strip of material. To judge from some civilian sculptures, such as that of Apinosus from Nièvre, this could be about 1.70m long. Fuentes suggested the possibility of different scarf colours providing a distinction between Cohorts and Legions, he also postulated that legionaries recruited from amongst marines may also have retained a blue scarf as a memory of their origins.

Waistband *(Fascia Ventralis)*
While the cummerbund of today is of Persian or

A reconstruction of military boots of the First century AD showing the hob-nails on the sole to protect the leather from wearing away. The method of lacing produced a ridge effect visible on grave *stelae*.

Opposite.
First century AD belt and apron, a reconstruction including belt plates from Rheingonheim and Oberstrimm.

Indian origin, a similar waist band was almost certainly known by the Romans. In fact a warrior on an Etruscan Cinerary urn from Volterra and the Celtic warrior from Avignon also appear to wear a band of material around the waist both of which suggest it could be worn with mail. A waist band can be seen on a statuette of a Lar, a household God, from Pompeii. A fresco also from Pompeii, in the house of the Vettii, shows two other Lares wearing the same type of sash. The purple red colour of the sash contrasts with the white tunic and a similar colour scheme may have been adopted by off duty soldiers. A fresco of Christian worshippers in the villa at Lullingstone shows these figures apparently wearing a waist band not unlike that of those from Pompeii. Like the Pompeii examples, the waist band on the Lullingstone figures is also a contrasting colour.

A study of Roman military grave stelae such as those belonging to P. Flavoleius Cordus from LEGIO XIII and Annaius of COHORS IIII DELMATARUM seem to indicate the existence of a waist sash, termed by Ubl a *Fascia Ventralis*, worn beneath the military belt. The best example of this is indicated on the torso

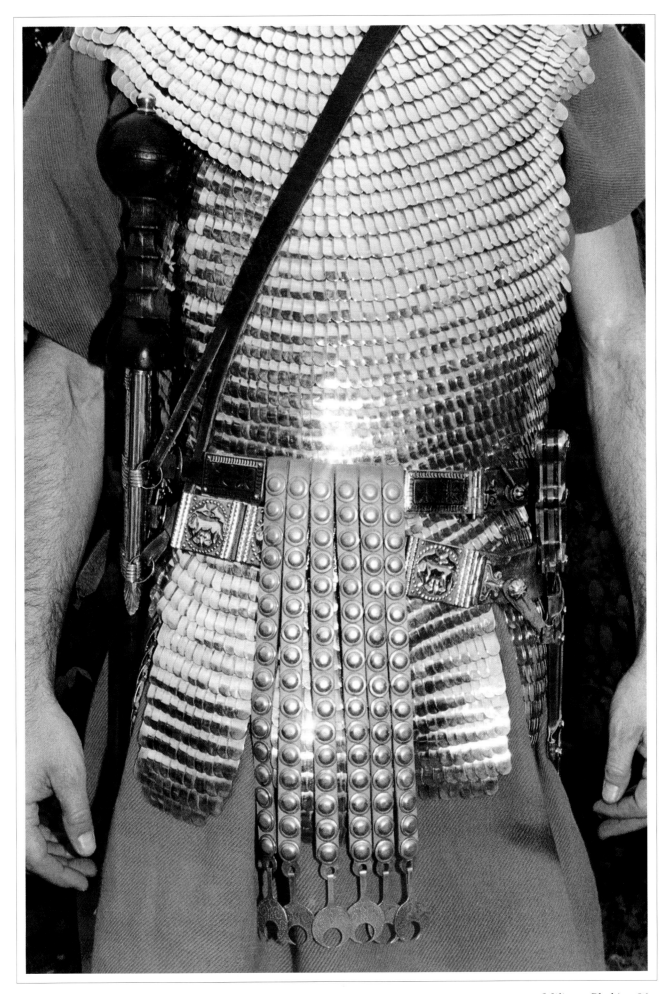

of a sculptured military figure from Casacco, in Northern Italy. Frequently associated with this waist sash is the depiction of a rectangular item tucked into the belt. This is often referred to in the case of the Auxilia as their discharge diplomas but as legionaries have them too it is suggested they are likely to be a set of writing tablets or even a leather purse. The numerous folds that appear on these bands may imply it was made from a length of fine material, such as linen. While the evidence for the existence of a waist sash remains speculative it would make the wearing of a belt far more comfortable as well as further enhancing the significance of this piece of equipment peculiar to the military.

Boots (*Caligae*)

By the First century AD, the standard military boot was the *Caliga*. When *Caligae* were first introduced into the Roman army remains unclear. On most sculptures of Republican soldiers they appear to be barefoot, but of course details such as boot straps could have been added in paint. There are references to boots in early Roman literature but these invariably refer to the enclosed boots worn by either senators or patricians coloured black or scarlet.

Studs and belt buckle Third century AD.

Caligae were constructed from three layers of vegetable tanned ox or cow hide, the tanning process itself incidentally took two years to complete. The boot consisted of an upper, an insole and a sole. The three layers were then clenched firmly with iron hob nails. The Grewelthorpe finds included a woollen insole implying a temporary repair. An indication that boots did wear away quite quickly is highlighted by an Egyptian papyrus stating that soldiers were issued with new pairs of boots and socks, three times a year. Once the nails started to wear through the leather, the boot was simply discarded, accounting for the large number of excavated examples especially from waterlogged sites. The upper is well ventilated as it is pierced with an open work design, which often leads to the boot being referred to as sandals. Although this open-work looks fragile it is deceptively strong. The straps can be laced up to suit the individual wearer while the ridge created by this lacing is often the only feature of the boot that was depicted on grave stelae.

Roman boot-makers clearly understood the principals of the distribution of weight of the foot during marching by their positioning of the hob nails on the insoles. Weight is initially placed on the heel and in modern reconstructions this is where the hob nails wear out first. Weight is then transferred diagonally towards the big toe. This movement of

weight is echoed by the pattern of nails underneath the boot. It has been remarked upon how these patterns fore-shadow modern computer designed sportswear. In turn these patterns can be further located to individual sites not only by surviving remains but the curious Roman habit of walking over wet roofing tiles as they were laid out to dry.

In spite of their highly functional design, *Caligae* disappear from use in the Second century AD. The army was either relying more and more on civilian contractors to produce military equipment or just following civilian fashions and the enclosed style of military boot used by the later army was no different from any other form of heavy duty footwear.

Belts *(Balteus)*

Wearing belts with mail armour served a practical function as well as a decorative one, as they helped take some of the weight off the shoulders. Two belts were often crossed over 'cowboy' fashion with one side arm suspended from each belt. This method of wearing belts changed during the course of the First century in favour of suspending the side arms from a single wider belt, it would seem this applied to both troops wearing a *Lorica Segmentata* as well as mail. There remained some instances of more than one belt being worn, which can be seen on a few tombstones and in one particular instance, on Trajan's Column a soldier wears four. When more than one belt is worn they are worn horizontally above one another.

Sculptures of Celtic belts or those apparently worn during the Republic were usually undecorated, although details could have been added in paint. Early Imperial belts, however, became another element that the individual soldier was able to decorate to his personal taste. The leather belt was covered with three types of metal plate, one ordinary, another with a hinged buckle and a third with a dagger frog attached. The sword has no need for frogs as it was either tied to the belt or suspended from a *baldric*. Evidence from Velsen suggests the plates did not completely encircle the belt, probably only covering the front. However in the case of the Herculaneum soldier there were enough belt plates found or implied to entirely cover his belts. As plates were tinned or silvered and covered with embossed or inlaid designs, cost might have been a limiting factor.

The plates on the belt belonging to Centurion M. Favonius Facilis, shown on his tombstone from Colchester, are larger than most contemporary examples. One plausible explanation is that it was easier to sculpt at a bigger size, while the floral design on his plates might simply be poorly represented cross

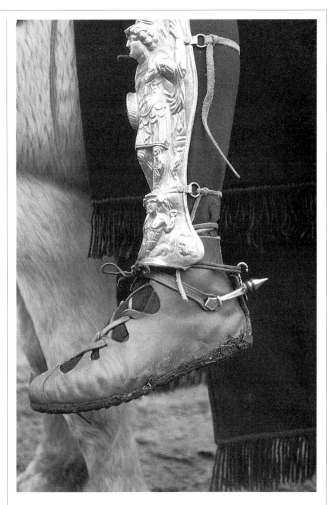

Detail of the later style of military boot in use from the Second century AD onwards. This view also shows a greave based on one from the Straubing hoard and a Roman spur. Part of the equipment reconstructed for the Archaeological Park Carnuntum.

motifs, one of the most common patterns in use. Second century belt fittings were completely different, many incorporating Celtic inspired open-work designs, these later developed into the elaborate *baldric* fittings of the Third century. Other examples included enamelled or *millefiori* inlaid plates.

Tombstones from the Third century often show a simple belt with a front fastening ring buckle. Belt ends appear to have been passed through the ring from behind the back along the front where they were fastened to metal studs on either side. In an echo of earlier times and how the early Imperial apron may have originally developed, an overhanging strap is seen on the wearers right. This strap was even fitted with one or two tear-drop terminals.

Rectangular buckles are also found at this period. Rectangular enamelled open-work plates are known on sites from both ends of the Empire. One set of rectangular plates from South Shields were interlocked by small chains.

Battle of Lyons, 197 AD

The painting opposite depicts a scene from the battle in which the Danubian army of Septimus Severus defeated the Western army of Clodius Albinus, Governor of Britain.

The *Lorica Segmentata* of early Imperial times seems to have largely disappeared by this date although some suits may still have been retained. Old fashions in armour, scale and mail have reappeared as standard equipment but in slightly modified form. Scale armour as worn by the Western legionary on the left is now more rigid. The individual pieces are wired to each of the four surrounding scales. Also, the pieces are longer, narrower and smaller than before. Another new feature are the embossed bronze breast plates usually described as cavalry parade armour. This is because of their elaborate nature but it was often the Roman soldiers practice to decorate even the most mundane and functional pieces of equipment. These breast plates protecting the front neck openings of otherwise fairly bland Cuirasses of scale and indeed mail, presented just such an opportunity. A number of these plates are in fact marked with legionary inscriptions and it is quite possible that they were intended to replace the old type of mail fasteners which now disappear from the archaeological record.

To save on cost, the legionary's scale Cuirass is fairly short and doesn't extend down his arms. Therefore the soldier wears an undergarment with leather *Pteruges* attached at the shoulder and hips to make up for this deficiency. This Western legionary wears what was described by Robinson as the best and most exciting legionary helmet to survive. The Niedermörmter helmet made completely of bronze with applied ornament which had been soldered in place was the last in the long line of Italic helmets that stretched back nearly two hundred years.

Around the waist he wears a leather belt to which are applied bronze tinned lettering spelling out the motto 'Use with good luck', perhaps rather inappropriate on this occasion for these belts may have been of Danubian origin and therefore possible acquired by this soldier in the initial victorious encounter of the army of Albinus over the forces of Severus. They were found in a burial at Lyon and may have been lost by one of the soldiers who fought in the second clash between the two armies.

The Danubian legionary on the right wears one of the new style mail shirts. They are much longer in the hips than earlier types and the use of *Pteruges* is unnecessary. His iron and bronze helmet was once classed as a cavalry helmet but very similar ones appear on infantry tombstones and it is now believed there was no difference between many cavalry and infantry helmets at this date.

Both infantrymen now wear leg breeches and enclosed boots. While the use of oval shields is now widespread, rectangular shields like the *Lorica Segmentata* may still have been retained by some units. Swords are now of the larger *Spatha* design and are worn on the left side. Daggers, once thought to have disappeared from use in the Second century AD, reappear in the early Third century, if indeed they ever dropped out of fashion. Daggers are now wider and longer than their earlier counterparts but the scabbards were much slender in form. A large hoard of over 50 of these daggers was found at Künzing in Germany. The broken standard belonged to LEGIO XX one of the British based Legions which would have formed the core of Albinus' army.

The cavalryman is a *Contarius* from one of the specialist units who used a *Contus,* a long lance type weapon. Like the scabbard slide of the Severan infantryman, the *Contus* was also of Sarmatian influence. The cavalryman wears a long mail shirt over a long sleeved tunic, a fashion that over the next few years was to become universal, he also has simple iron *greaves* on his legs. Just as the Italic infantry helmet was one of the last of its kind, the same distinctions can be applied to this iron and bronze cavalry helmet. In this particular instance it is one of the most elaborate of its kind. Yellow crests are often associated with cavalry because of a reference by the soldier historian, Arrian, while green saddlecloths are known from two separate sources two hundred years apart. Circular *phalerae* and *lunate* pendants are depicted on late Second century sculpture, such as figures from the columns of Antoninus and Marcus Aurelius, while the horse's mane is tied up in a fashion highlighted on a tombstone of a *Contarius* from Tipasa in Algeria. Painting by Graham Turner.

Weapons and Equipment

Swords (*Gladius* and Spatha)

Mention has already been made of a possible change in fighting techniques from the late Republic to that of the early Empire. The possibility that Roman soldiers adopted a more upright posture as opposed to a crouched one may even have affected one of the most famous weapons ever used, the *Gladius* or short stabbing sword.

Although Celtic warriors are more often associated with the long slashing sword, most commentators ancient and modern state that the origins of the *Gladius* derived from contact with Celtic warriors in Spain, indeed the *Gladius* is often referred to as the *Gladius Hispaniensis* (Spanish sword). By the reign of

Augustus, a sword termed the *Mainz* type after the discovery of large quantities of swords in the Rhine, was probably fairly widespread. *Mainz* swords had a blade of varying widths from 48 to 75mm and a length of 400 mm to 550mm. These swords are distinguished by their long tapering points and are therefore described as an ideal stabbing weapon. In addition these swords appear to have slightly curved edges which may have been caused by repeated sharpening otherwise it would have no obvious function.

The later Roman historian Vegetius mentions how the Romans scorned those who used slashing strokes.

A legionary supply wagon from the arch of Severus.

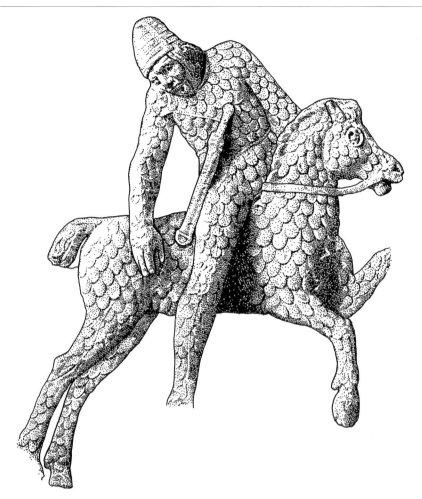

The image of Romans stabbing upwards into the stomachs or armpits of the upwardly raised right arm of their Celtic opponents has entered modern day mythology. But according to the Greek historian Polybius, the Roman 'Spanish sword' could be used for chopping as well as stabbing, so as with many aspects of the Roman Army there is always room for alternative explanations.

The *Mainz* type swords were provided with scabbards renowned for their elaborate fittings, some superb examples of which have been recovered. These have been divided into three categories. The earliest scabbard from Mainz has complex open-work fittings at its mouth and chape. Other comparable examples have been dated from between 15BC and at least AD 45. The so called 'sword of Tiberius' was also a *Mainz* type sword but in this case the open-work has been replaced by embossed designs including an image of the Emperor. This highly decorated piece has been considered as a gift from the Emperor for some military achievement, but as has been seen elsewhere, most Roman equipment was often very elaborate, even items belonging to the lowest class of soldier. The 'sword of Tiberius' should perhaps be seen as typical rather than unusual. *Mainz* swords were almost totally encased with embossed plates, a prime example of

which is the 'Fulham Sword', while another spectacular version comes from Strasbourg. Both the 'Fulham sword' and the 'sword of Tiberius' were constructed by having soft low carbon iron sandwiched between the carbonised steel strips and additionally they may have been quenched. Recent analysis concluded these swords were generally of a higher quality than those which appeared later.

Roman troops in Britain during the early invasion period may well have used swords which owed more in design to those of their Briton opponents than to the army they fought for. These 'native' swords have been found on a couple of sites and while they have some affinities with contemporary Roman swords their overall appearance harks back to iron age Celtic swords. Certainly by the time of the destruction of Pompeii in AD 79, a completely new type of sword had been introduced. Four swords were found during excavations of this famous site, known today as the *Pompeii* pattern. The only positively identified Roman

Reconstructions of Third century AD baldric fittings. The round *Phalerae* is based on an example from Carlisle, while the rectangular hinged terminal plate and terminal pendant are copies of finds from Zugmantel. Archaeological Park Carnuntum.

Third century sword and baldric fittings. The ring pommel on the sword and scabbard suspension slide were probably introduced into the Roman army through contact with the Sarmatians. The baldric fitting resembles the standards carried by *Beneficiarii* and may therefore be another badge of office used by these soldiers. Other possible devices representing *Beneficiarii* are terminal straps which also have the standard motif. Archaeological Park Carnuntum.

sword from the Republican period shows more of the characteristics of these *Pompeii* swords than the early *Mainz* type, which suggests it had an earlier origin.

The possibility of a change in fighting techniques regarded as influential in helmet and armour changes may have been responsible for the change in the shape of swords, but definite evidence for *Pompeii* pattern swords appearing as early as the new Gallic and Italic helmets is lacking. This does not rule out the possibility of the evidence being found one day. We should remember that the *Lorica Segmentata* was not believed to have been introduced until the Claudian period, until finds dating to the Augustan period were excavated.

Pompeii swords had parallel edges with a shorter stabbing point. They average between 42 and 55mm in width and have a length averaging from 420 to 500mm. The *Pompeii* sword would seem ideally suited for both stabbing or chopping at close quarters. Like the early *Mainz* type scabbards, *Pompeii* sword scabbards had decorated mouths and chapes. The

mouth pieces were often tinned or silvered with punched out shapes and inscribed details usually taking the form of deities. Scabbard sheaths were usually made of wood covered with leather.

Roman cavalry of the early Empire used a longer sword commonly known as the *Spatha*. It was almost certainly developed from Celtic swords. Its length enabled the cavalryman to reach an enemy on foot, and the long parallel sides were perfectly suited as a slashing weapon. To give some idea of the length of these weapons, one sword from Rottweil was 865mm long and 44mm wide compared with another from Newstead which was only 622mm long and 25mm

Opposite.
Reconstruction of a *Mainz* type sword and scabbard from the early Imperial period.

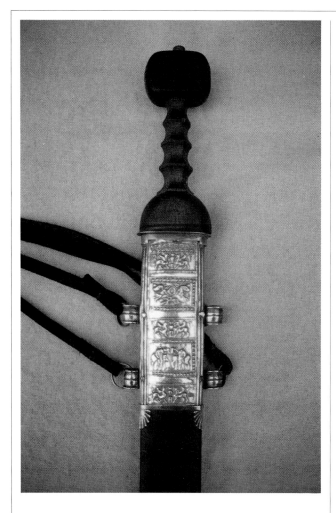

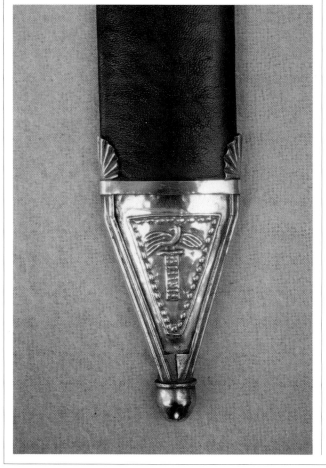

wide. Like some of the infantry swords, a *Spatha* from Augst had been quenched and tempered for strength.

Two Roman *Spatha* swords were found in a double inhumation burial excavated in Canterbury. It appeared the two skeletons were aged between 20 and 30. The grave was quite small and the taller man had his legs pulled backwards to fit into the grave. The date of the burial suggests a late First or Second century date but it is very unusual for weapons to be included along with a burial. Remains of the scabbards and sheaths were found on both swords. One had an iron *Peltate Chape*, the other bronze. One of the swords had a poplar and willow grip and a contrasting maple wood guard while those on the other sword were entirely of maple. Whereas the *Gladius* underwent several developments in its history, the few remaining examples of *Spathas* would seem to indicate that its basic shape remained unaltered. From the Third century onwards it would become the standard weapon of both cavalry and infantry.

A new form of the *Gladius* appeared in the Second century, where the iron tang previously covered with a wooden pommel and guard became an integral part of the hand guard with the pommel becoming a ring. Ring pommel swords trace their ancestry back to Trans-Danubian tribes like the Sarmatians and contact with these people from the Dacian wars onwards brought new forms of equipment into the Roman army. After this period, scabbards were less elaborate than before, *Peltate Chapes* like those from Canterbury or semi circular ones replaced the triangular shapes of earlier forms. Instead of side suspension rings, scabbards were now suspended from a belt passing through a scabbard slide. These scabbard slides often took the form of dolphins, perhaps symbolising swiftness and speed. This method of attaching swords that appears to have originated with the Sarmatians.

Although *Pompeii* type swords disappear in the Third century, short swords may have had some continued use. One example from Künzing had a triangular tapering point 400mm long. Third century swords were provided with a variety of grips and guards. Archaeological evidence exists for plain, ribbed or fluted grips with iron or copper alloy guards. Pommels were generally more elliptical than before but sarcophagii and tombstones also show Pommels with eagle heads. Circular *Chapes* are depicted on a number of Third century tombstones. Existing finds are of ivory, bone copper alloy or even iron ones which were also inlaid with coloured metals. These

Reconstructed Cavalry *Spatha* Scabbard based on finds from Pettau, showing strong Thracian influences.

Chapes survived into the Third century while box *Chapes* of bone or copper alloy were an alternative.

The sword was now suspended by a broad *baldric*. This was probably leather and was decorated with Circular *Phalera* and rectangular and ivy leaf pendant plates. Circular *Phalera* were either plain, decorated with patterns or open-work designs. The Eagle of Jupiter was a common feature of these designs. The rectangular plates and ivy leaf pendants could also be of the same open-work design as some of the *Phalera* and could therefore make up an attractive set.

Pila and Spears

Before the Roman infantryman charged with his short stabbing sword he threw the *Pila*, heavy or lighter javelins in murderous volleys. The most famous feature of this weapon was its ability to bend on impact, making it impractical to throw back. However its prime function was as an armour piercing weapon which can be seen by its heavy pyramidal bodkin-head, which in modern experiments is capable of penetrating 30mm of pine wood from a distance of 5m. Therefore a *Pilum* could easily pierce an enemy shield and with its long shank would be carried beyond into the enemy's body, probably forcing its way through his armour as well. Sculpture suggests that extra weights were added, presumably to give extra penetration. Caesar recorded another benefit of this action, for if an enemy advanced with over-lapping shields, the *Pilum* would pierce them both, pinning them together, thus disabling two shields at once. More well known is the fact that the soft iron shank would bend after impact denying its use to the enemy. According to the historian Plutarch this was occasionally assisted by attaching the shank to the wooden shaft by at least one wooden rivet. Re-enactors have been able to duplicate this bending action of the *Pilum* quite successfully.

Examples of Republican *Pila* have a head about 60mm long with a shank 554mm in length. Well preserved Imperial *Pila* from Oberaden where even parts of the wooden staff survived were over 700mm in total length. An alternative and lighter weapon was achieved when the shank was socketed as opposed to riveted to the shaft. *Pila* were probably fitted with a butt, therefore while the soldier threw one weapon he could have another close to hand, stuck into the ground. A *Pilum* on the Cancellaria relief is definitely

Details of a cavalry *Spatha* scabbard based on a find from Rottweil. The bottom plate survived in a fragmentary state but the upper locket plates have been reconstructed using contemporary *gladius* plates reproducing the inlaid Mars figure that was visible in the lower plate.

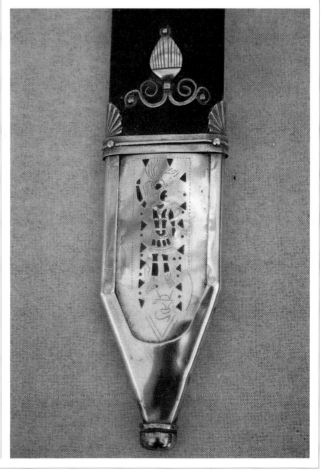

Reconstruction of the First century AD *Mainz* type sword and scabbard found in the River Thames at Fulham.

fitted with a butt. Some form of binding appears on the shaft on some sculptures as well as indications of the possibility of a throwing thong. *Pila* had a long history of use in the Roman army. Perhaps even dating back as far as the Fourth century BC. Although its origins are obscure, with slight variations it remained in use throughout the period covered by this book. A later variant with a barbed head was almost certainly developed from a Germanic spear which was itself probably a barbarian version of the Roman *Pilum*.

The majority of Roman spearheads were of the 'leaf shaped' variety which come in a number of sizes. 'Leaf shaped' spears called *hastae* were in continuous use by Auxiliary infantry and cavalry and increasingly as the Imperial era wore on by legionaries too. Larger spear heads were perhaps most useful as stabbing weapons, while the shorter headed weapons were probably for throwing. Those that fall between these two very broad categories may have had a dual function, unfortunately little experimentation has

Reconstructed scabbard and suspension slide Third century AD.

taken place to prove this conclusively. It would be difficult to fight effectively at close quarters carrying more than one throwing spear, so the handful of sculptures showing soldiers with more than one spear may well represent javelins. A Third century grave *stela* from Apamea shows a Trainee Javelineer or *Lanciarius* carrying five leaf shaped spears possibly in a quiver.

Experiments have been carried out with throwing javelins based on a type found at South Shields. A blade 140mm in length was attached to a shaft made from ash, although poplar, willow, and alder were other types of wood that could be used in javelin shafts. The head was attached by means of a small nail through a hole in the head socket. During the course of the experiments if any spear shafts snapped they did so at the point of fastening. This, together with the fact that the blade itself frequently bent, meant it would be difficult to reuse these weapons under battle conditions, but afterwards it would require only minor repairs to restore damaged spear heads. Reconstructed

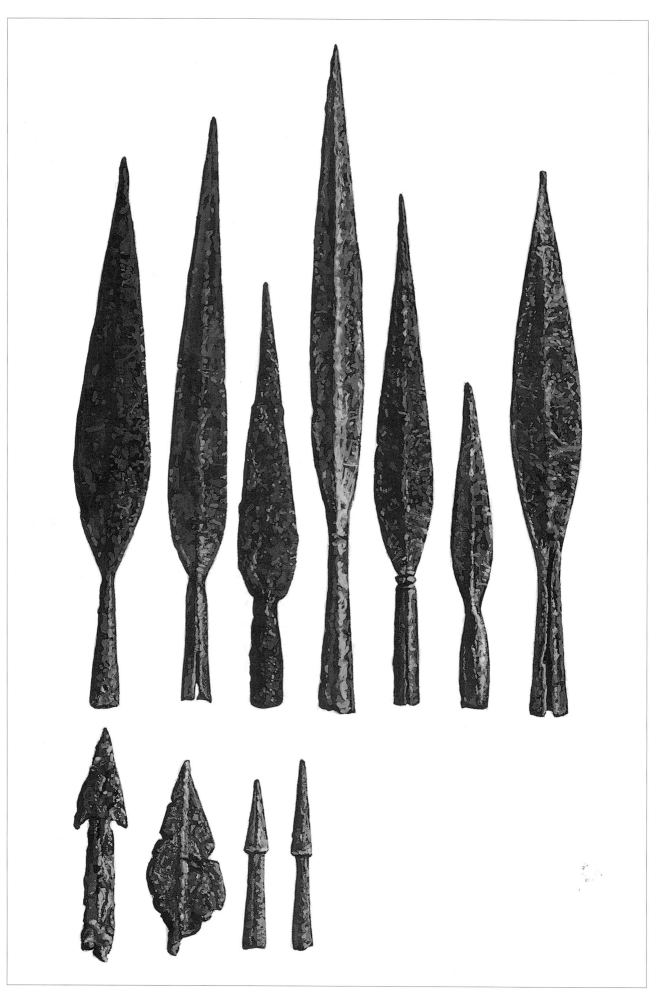

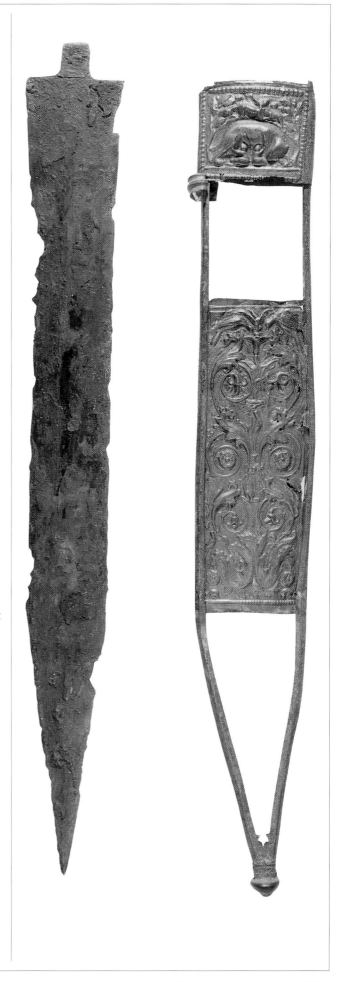

javelins easily pierced wooden shields at a depth of
18mm from a distance of 10 metres. It was also
possible to throw five javelins at an attacker running
towards the thrower from a distance of 20 metres,
even allowing time for the javelin man to draw his
sword.

Experiments indicated that the javelins had a range
of at least 15-20m using javelins with shafts between
1.75 and 2m. Shafts over that length consistently
snapped at the base of the socket while those below,
became top heavy and equally ineffective. Similar
javelins have been used by cavalry re-enactors and the
effectiveness of light javelins was demonstrated when
they easily passed through straw dummy targets. This
was after some initial problems, one rider actually
overtook his dart in mid flight. Cavalry re-enactors
have also used the longer shafted spears in the manner
of a lance and, as demonstrated on many Roman
tombstones, executed with an overhand method. Used
overhand the spears prove to be very effective against
an infantryman, as it gives the rider the ability to hit
him in the front or back or reach him on the ground.
An idea of some of the punching power available is
that even with a padded leather tip, on one occasion a
spear went straight through a plywood shield.

Daggers

Possibly encountered during the wars in Spain the
dagger was adopted as an additional sidearm during
the late Republic. Initially with a round Pommel, a flat
headed version first appeared during the Augustan
period and this 'T' shape handle became a familiar
feature of Roman equipment. Daggers were used by
both legionaries and Auxiliaries as evidenced by their
tombstones. Cavalrymen too may have owned them
but so far there is only literary evidence to support
this. In effect the dagger was a smaller version of the
Mainz type sword, and is frequently found with
grooves running the length of the blade. These
grooves were possibly a means of introducing air in to
a wound, which would suggest the dagger was more
than just a tool to be used around the camp. In fact
there were plenty of other items of equipment
available to the Roman soldier for small scale craft-

**First century AD 'Fulham' sword now in the British Museum.
This shows the long tapering blade of the Mainz type swords.
Romulus and Remus being suckled by the she wolf can be
seen on the top plate of the Scabbard.** © British Museum.

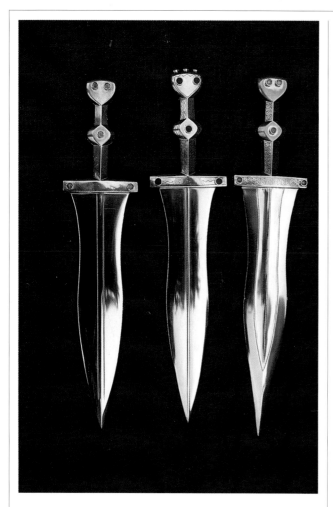

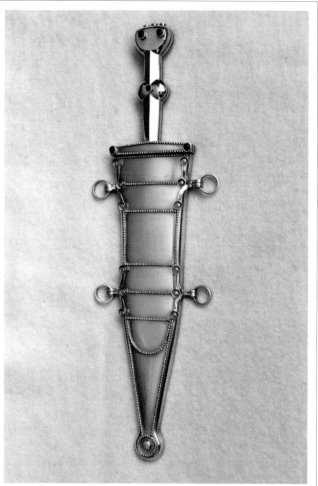

A selection of reconstructed dagger blades from the First century AD made by Martin White of the *Ermine Street Guard*. The central example with the three rivets on the handle top can be seen on a contempory tombstone. Ridges and grooves added to the blade increased its strength.

Reconstructed dagger and scabbard based on a find from Leiden dating to the First century AD.

work.

Most items of Roman equipment were decorated to some degree, but it is the dagger scabbard that the individual soldiers paid most attention to. Two basic types of scabbard have been identified, the first was constructed from two iron plates which were joined at the edges with an internal wooden lining. The second type was made from organic materials mostly of leather or wood with a single metal plate attached at the front. In some cases traces of the wooden lining still adheres to the dagger. Four suspension rings were then riveted to the scabbard. Some of the early scabbards are surprisingly undecorated. These were once believed to be the standard issues that were later replaced by personalised purchases. It seems more likely that these were the original designs that were introduced into the army.

The amount and nature of decorations on the dagger would appear to have been determined by the amount of money the soldier was prepared to pay.

Some of the more elaborate could therefore have belonged to junior officers. Decoration comes in a variety of geometric or even Celtic designs, which were often inlaid with silver, brass, ivory, coloured enamels and niello. A common belief was that daggers declined in use in the Second century but this does not seem to have been the case. Although simple in design and with less decorated sheaths, daggers are still found up to the Third century and were evidently considered a useful and necessary item of equipment.

Hand hurled Stones

The Roman army utilised all of the available weapons technology that was known to the ancient world, from the humblest thrown stone to sophisticated artillery machines. All soldiers were probably trained to us a variety of weapons, but also units which specialised in the use of a particular weapon were created.

Greek armies employed *Thracian* stone throwers

Opposite.
A reconstructed First century cavalryman about to throw a replica javelin.

called *Psiloi* to considerable effect. Even if not killed outright an armoured man might still be knocked senseless by hand hurled stones and made vulnerable. Greek vases show a number of *Psiloi*, they are un-armoured and protected only occasionally by a simple shield. In appearance this is not unlike a figure depicted on Trajan's Column although this is generally regarded as an artistic error. Stone throwers would be particularly useful defending a fortified position. Large numbers of orange sized stones have been found on military sites usually with a flattened side which would make them easy to stack. Although these are usually interpreted as artillery shot, they could equally well have been hand thrown stones. Experiments carried out with hand hurled stones at the reconstructed fort gateway at South Shields achieved some convincing results. Even novice throwers were able to obtain a high degree of accuracy over an average distance of 24.31m. More importantly the action required to hurl a stone to the base of the wall, exposed less of the body than firing a bow or throwing a javelin.

Slings

Of all the weapons used by the Roman army the sling is perhaps one of the hardest to study, due to the high degree of skill that is required to use it. Modern experiments where the shot flew out at all angles, including upwards and backwards, conjures up images of the dangers faced when training large numbers of raw recruits. It does not come as a surprise, however, to discover that the Romans recruited specialist slingers from areas with long standing traditions in using this weapon. The Balearic Islands is one such area where the use of the sling continued into modern times.

While the sling itself was probably of an organic material and therefore not likely to leave any trace, the type of shot used survives on many Roman sites. Clay shot is quite common although just as likely to have been used against the Romans as by them. Lead walnut-shaped shot was exclusively Greco-Roman. During the Civil Wars of the late Republic lead shot often had stamped political messages or simple slogans like 'Take That'. Pompey's soldiers found it prudent to wear extra wicker coverings over their helmets as protection against sling shot. Slings were also useful against elephants and in the medical treatise, *De Medicina*, Celsus recorded how a slingshot wound was more dangerous and harder to treat than one inflicted by an arrow.

A number of slingers are depicted on Trajan's Column, like the possible stone thrower they are un-

Aurelius Mucianus, a trainee *lanciarius* who died at Apamea early in the Third century AD, while serving with LEGIO II PARTHICA. The *lancea* would appear to have been a small throwing spear with a leaf shaped head, possibly carried in a quiver which may be intended on the sculpture. Other features that highlight the difficulties of interpretation from sculptured monuments are the small round shield which maybe artistic licence, and that Mucianus appears to be wearing socks rolled down over his boots.

armoured and equally likely to be an artistic measure to stress the cosmopolitan nature of the army. The widespread nature of slingshot finds would suggest that as well as the specialist units, slingers were made up from small detachments of men trained from within any unit who would therefore wear regular equipment. Indeed Hadrianus in his speech to the army of Africa mentions the use of slings by the cavalrymen in COHORS VI COMMAGENORUM EQ.

Archery

Archery was another field in which the Romans recruited from amongst experienced people, especially the Eastern regions. Like slingers, it is possible they were equipped as regular infantry or cavalry rather

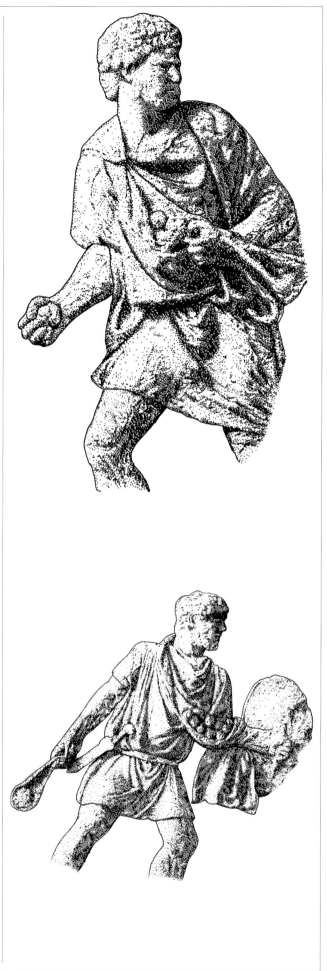

Top.
An officer with an eagle pommelled sword on a relief from Brincovenesti.

Top right.
Stone thrower from Trajan's Column.

Bottom right.
Roman slinger from Trajan's Column.

than as their exotic appearance on Trajan's Column would indicate. Certainly First century tombstones depict archers in the usual off duty uniform of tunic with sword and dagger belts. Also likely is the possibility that individual soldiers within any given unit acquired the necessary ability to use bows and arrows, rather than simply having to rely on specialist units. Composite bows constructed from sinew and wood with stiffeners of bone or iron were the standard type of bow in use in the ancient world. Notched stiffeners are usually the only surviving evidence of the bow but arrowheads are frequently found. Archers would also have required the use of a leather bracer on the left forearm and details of these are shown on Trajan's Column.

Arrowheads come in three categories mainly

Reconstructed Dagger and Scabbard, First century AD, based on evidence from Hod Hill in Dorset.

tanged, although the Romans also employed socketed types as well. These are of the flat bladed and triple bladed type as well as those designed to carry incendiary material. During modern experiments socketed arrows tended to break behind the socket like the replica javelins. Whether this action was deliberately intended or simply as an accidental by-product of manufacture is hard to ascertain. *Tanged* arrowheads proved less likely to break on impact, but the binding required to hold the head in place limited their degree of penetration. These experiments were used against most of the known forms of Roman armour and only the *Lorica Segmentata* proved to be completely effective. Somewhat surprisingly the wooden shield, especially if covered with leather, almost provided as much defence.

Staffs, Sticks and Clubs

Part of a Centurion's badge of office was his twisted vine stick (*vitis*), but other sticks or wooden clubs were used by Roman troops. The *vitis* is shown on a number of surviving tombstones held in the right hand. Its use was not just ceremonial, as attested by the famous account of one of Tiberius's Centurions, Lucilius. Lucilius earned the sobriquet 'Cedo Alteram' (bring me another) from his soldiers, because of his habit of breaking his *vitis* over soldiers backs and shouting for another and another. This had unfortunate and fatal consequences for Lucilius for during a mutiny in AD14 he was one of the first targets for retribution.

Another soldier who carried a stick as an emblem of office was the Centurion's deputy, the *Optio*. Caecilius Avitus, an *Optio* of LEGIO XX from Chester, is depicted on his grave stelae with his staff. It is taller than he is and is finished with a knobbed end which is often interpreted as being metal. Like the *vitis*, this staff may also have had a practical function, one possibility would be to keep troops in line while on the march by knocking or pushing them into position. Other soldiers were picked out of the ranks for special policing duties, therefore freeing them from the more routine and unpleasant tasks. This benefit was recognised by these soldiers bearing the official title *Beneficiarius*. To further distinguish these soldiers they too carried a staff, topped with an elaborate spear head. These spear heads exhibit such fashions as silvering, copper alloy inlays, circular perforations, and attached rings.

The *Beneficarii* lance could be used to cordon off a particular area, as a security measure for instance. Long strips of material could be attached to the lance to make a barrier for which it would be an offence for any unauthorised individual to cross. One tombstone from Apamea appears to show these straps attached to a *Beneficarius* lance.

Sometimes confused with the *vitis*, another clubbed stick carried by ordinary soldiers and *Beneficarii* was the *Fustis*. The *Fustis* could be used for effective crowd control just as riot police use them today. One such instance occurred during the Governorship of Pontius Pilate, Prefect of Judaea, when his troops disguised as citizens mingled with the crowd. On a given signal they revealed wooden sticks hidden beneath their cloaks by which they dispersed the crowd, killing and injuring many. On grave stelae the soldiers carrying a *Fustis* hold it like a club.

Simple wooden clubs were occasionally used in battle too. At last one tombstone of a Briton holding a large club exists, while Trajan's Column again depicts a barbarian auxiliary wielding one in a battle scene. Palestinian auxiliaries armed only with clubs were able to defeat heavily armoured cataphract cavalry simply by clubbing them to death.

Shields (Scutum)

A general misconception shared by many members of the public is that the Roman shield was made entirely of metal. It is a great surprise therefore when they discover they were constructed by a method which today we would call plywood. According to the Roman historian Livy the curved oblong shield that was to become a mainstay of Roman equipment was introduced in the Fourth century BC. With minor developments this same basic design was still in use in the Third century AD, before it was finally replaced by a large oval shield.

Our main source of evidence for the early appearance of this shield are two representations on the alter of Domitius Ahenobarbus, and the monument of Aemilius Paullus plus a description by the Greek historian Polybius. Polybius describes a shield constructed out of two layers of wood which were stuck together with bull's hide glue. This was then covered with canvas and calf skin. To protect the edges of the wood from splitting, the top and bottom of the shield were edged with metal. The central horizontal hand grip was protected by an iron boss which as Polybius described also deflected stones, spears and other missiles. The hand-grip could also be reinforced by metal bars.

The shield Polybius describes is remarkably similar to a well preserved example found at Kasr-el-Harit in the Fayum district of Egypt although this shield has often been referred to as an earlier Ptolemaic shield possibly belonging to a Celtic mercenary. The Kasr-el-Harit shield was 1.28m long and .635m wide. Unlike the shield mentioned by Polybius, it had three layers of wooden strips probably of birch wood. The shield was so constructed it was thicker nearer the centre than the edges, therefore a blow striking the front would deflect to the outside.

The shield was further strengthened by a vertical wooden rib and a 'barleycorn' shaped wooden boss although metal bosses which conform in size and shape have been discovered elsewhere. The curvature at the top edge allowed the soldier to glance around but otherwise if the Roman soldier crouched behind these shields, as suggested by Connolly, he was fully protected from the ankle to the head. Reliefs on the Arch of Orange in Southern France dating to the reign of Augustus show this shield was still in use by then, but then soon after, like so much other Roman equipment, modification began to take place. These reliefs also record motifs on the shield in the form of eagle's wings. Polybius's quite detailed description makes no mention of any kind of emblem being painted on the shield, nor are they seen on the

A reconstruction of a dagger and scabbard, Third century AD based on a find from London.

monument of Aemilius Paulus, although the Greek adversaries on this relief clearly have decorated shields. It has been suggested that designs were not introduced until the Civil Wars at the end of the Republic.

By the First century AD, to judge from the evidence both sculptural and archaeological, a number of different shaped shields had been introduced. One source of evidence is actually the leather coverings from these shields which may survive even if the rest of the shield does not. A leather shield cover from the fortress of LEGIO II AUGUSTA at Caerleon provided a completely unknown shield shape, straight sided with rounded edges. Another leather cover from Castleford in Yorkshire, belonged almost certainly to a small circular shield, which are depicted on Trajan's Column being carried by standard bearers. When circular shields are attached to a leather strap and carried over the shoulder, they almost naturally tuck under the left arm, an attitude perfectly captured on the column itself. Considering their rarity in any particular unit it was quite a surprise when archaeologists discovered remains of a second circular cover at the same site.

112 *Weapons and Equipment*

Top.
A barbarian armed with a club from a scene on Trajan's Column.

Top right.
An irregular archer from the column.

Bottom right.
An Auxiliary archer wearing standard equipment from Trajan's Column.

Shield bosses for legionary shields are rare finds and like the shield itself were rectangular and curved, flat circular bosses presumably from Auxiliary shields are more common. Bosses could be either of punched iron or of copper alloy which would be spun. Surprisingly for a piece of equipment that was likely to receive considerable damage, some bosses, like the example from the River Tyne lost or deposited by a soldier from LEGIO VIII AUGUSTA, are inscribed

Opposite.
Balaterus, a soldier with COHORS VI DELMATARUM stationed in Mauretania around 40 AD. He wears a *Sagum* cloak and carries two spears and a stick *Fustis* in his right hand used like a riot police baton.

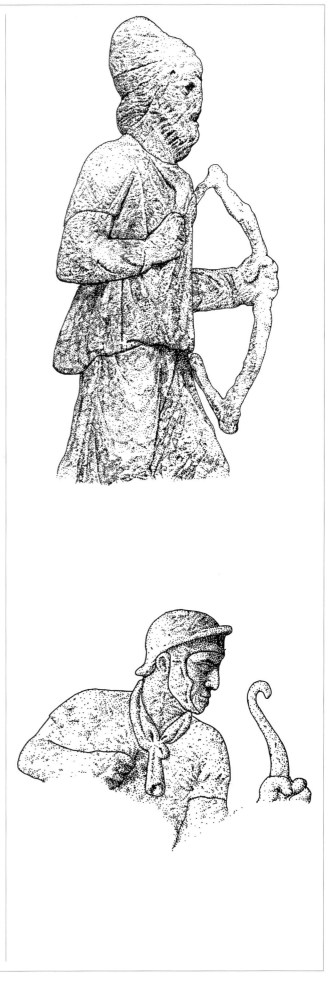

With the crouched fighting stance of the Augustan infantryman the shield practically covered the entire body.

Side view of a reconstructed eastern Auxiliary archer showing the shape of the composite bow when drawn.

with decorations. All the evidence available strongly leads one to the conclusion, that the curved rectangular shields were exclusively used by the legionaries and the flat shields were the equipment of the Auxilia. Two tombstones of legionaries, P. Flavoleius Cordus of LEGIO XIIII GEMINA and C. Castricius Victor of LEGIO II ADIUTRIX both depict oval shields, normally associated with the Auxilia, although like the rectangular shields they may have been curved. Apart from an Auxiliary COHORS SCUTATA which may have been equipped with a legionary shield and an Auxiliary carrying a rectangular curved shield on Trajan's Column (an artistic error?), there is no evidence the Auxilia were equipped with anything other than flat shields, these were generally oval but some large flat rectangular shields appear on tombstones, and are suggested by finds of leather covers.

Auxiliary cavalry may have carried circular shields at the beginning of the Imperial era but all the First century tombstones show cavalrymen with oval rectangular or even hexagonal shields. Remains of a flat rectangular shield were recovered from a fort at

Doncaster in Yorkshire. This shield appeared to have an iron vertical hand grip which it was suggested by the excavator might have been easier to handle by someone who was mounted. However re-enactors have found the horizontal hand grip quite adequate. Furthermore the boss on the Doncaster shield was slightly above the centre of the shield which in its reconstruction affected its balance, making it tip towards the legs. This would be a nuisance to an infantryman on the march but would provide additional protection to a cavalryman.

Bronze 'U' shaped edging from shields are found on many Roman sites although the Doncaster shield had none at least when it was deposited. This edging, was attached to the shield with brass nails and inserted

Opposite.
Syrian archers with composite bows reconstructed exactly as depicted on Trajan's column, although recently doubt has been cast on this identification. Other archers including Easterners are shown elsewhere wearing standard Auxiliary equipment. Again this highlights the difficulties of basing reconstructions simply on sculptural evidence alone.

Opposite.
Restored suit of crocodile armour found in Egypt in the nineteenth century. © British Museum.

Left.
Third century wooden shield from Dura Europos, the design probably shows an eastern god or a Roman Emperor.

Below.
A sword and two shields from Gallic reliefs. One shield bears a marked resemblance to a design shown on Trajan's Column.

through lobate extensions regularly spaced at intervals along the edging. As well as the metal reinforces on the back of the shield, metal sheeting may have been applied to the front of many shields. The lightning device shown on many shield representations would have been an attractive and appropriate choice if picked out in bronze. Traces of sheet bronze was found on the Doncaster shield but it was not possible to determine the exact nature of the original design. The possibility of a combination of metal and painted designs on shields cannot be ruled out.

Reflecting the general concerns for more defective tactics and fighting, at some point in the Third century large oval shields generally replaced all the other forms, although smaller circular shields may

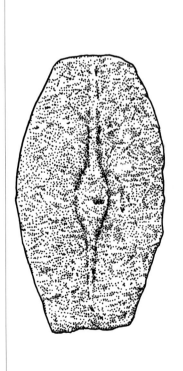
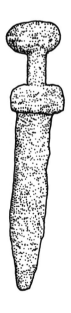
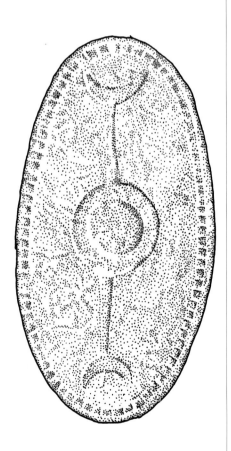

Palmyrenes clash with Romans in the Nile Delta, 269 AD

In 269, under the leadership of Queen Zenobia, the city state of Palmyra broke away from Roman rule, and quickly won control over most of the Eastern Empire. The Palmyrenes invaded Egypt and although out manoeuvred by Roman forces destroyed the Roman army in the Nile Delta.

The right foreground figure is an Egyptian levy in the Roman army, wearing a suit of crocodile armour based on a find from Manfalut in Egypt. Although both hippopotamus and crocodile armour is known to have existed, their use as battle equipment is considered somewhat controversial. More than one piece of crocodile armour survives but it is uncertain as to who used it or to what purpose. Crocodile skins may well have been worn in religious ceremonies, but another possibility is that they conceivably could have been used by the bandits which plagued Egypt in the Third century or as suggested here that they were pressed into service to equip hastily recruited levies in the face of the Palmyrene invasion.

The Egyptian warrior is attacking a Roman legionary from the army of Syria, formally under the command of Odenathus, the husband of Zenobia, until his death in 267. In an age of uncertain loyalties the actions of the eastern Legions remains unclear. However considering the practice of local recruitment amongst both legions and Auxiliary units, they may well have thrown in their lot with Zenobia.

The legionary is equipped with a large oval shield restored with a device found on a shield on Dura-Europos. He wears a bronze helmet based on a find from Germany although there was evidence for similar helmets at Dura-Europos. It has a deep neck guard, angled peak and crossed reinforces on the bowl. *A spatha* sword appears to have been the standard weapon for both foot and horse, however the *pilum* remained in use and a socketed version is illustrated here. Finally the legionary wears a suit of bronze mail. Iron mail shirts with devices made up of bronze rings are also known.

In the background is a Palmyrene camel rider. Evidence for this type of military figure is scarce but representations of Palmyrene gods on camel back are quite frequent and probably depict the sort of equipment in use. This includes small round shields, spears sometimes in a quiver and occasionally a composite bow. The gods are either fully armoured with a cuirass, possibly of lamellar armour modelled on Hellenistic lines, or un-armoured with a loose fitting robe sometimes gathered up between the legs. Helmets are rarely shown but this may have been an artistic convention.
Painting by Graham Turner.

Reconstructed legionaries advance in close formation giving an indication of how much protection the shields offered.

Left.

Highly decorated shield boss *umbo*. Such an item would once have been described as simply parade equipment, but the Roman propensity for decorating even the most humblest piece of equipment brings this into question. (Archaeological Park Carnuntum).

Bottom.

Decorated bronze plate belonging to a bolt shooting artillery machine operated by LEGIO IIII MACEDONICA and lost at the battle of Cremona in 69 AD. This piece was originally believed to have been part of a legionary pay chest.

have continued in use. At Dura-Europos in Syria twenty four complete or partially complete oval shields were discovered, including possibly the last piece of evidence for the rectangular shield. Compared with shields from earlier periods the overall effect of these shields is one of cheapness. Instead of the layers of wood the shields are constructed from twelve to fifteen poplar wooden planks. There are no metal reinforcing bars at the back and the hand grip is simply made by cut outs in the planks. Gone also is the metal edging replaced by a cruder, but nevertheless quite effective rawhide strip which was sewn on. Modern re-enactors seem to find dog chews a suitable substitute.

Top.
Larger than a *catapulta*, the *ballista* operated on the same principle but fired round shot instead of bolts. Sandstone shot over 30cm in diameter and weighing 4360g were found at Numantia, the site of a siege in Republican times. Larger stones are found at a number of sites but these could have been simply dropped from the walls by defenders. Equally some of the smaller shot may well have been for hand throwing. The use of artillery machines by the Auxilia is debatable, while there is evidence for the use of artillery on 'Auxiliary' sites, they could have been operated by legionary specialists.

Right.
Reconstruction of a small *catapulta,* up to sixty of these machines could be found in a single legion. Mounted on carts they could provide mobile artillery. Men were pinned to their horses or shot out of windows by bolts from these machines.

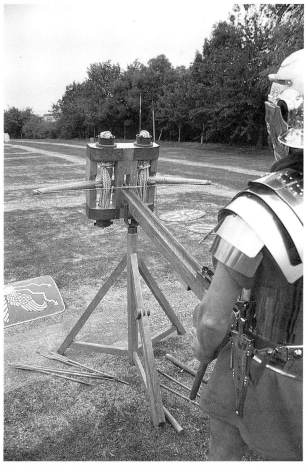

A number of different shield emblems both legionary and Auxiliary are shown on Trajan's Column, some of these correspond to those on other monuments. Efforts have even been made to connect these designs to particular units. Certain signs of the Zodiac are depicted on some shields and where these reflect known unit insignia there could well be a

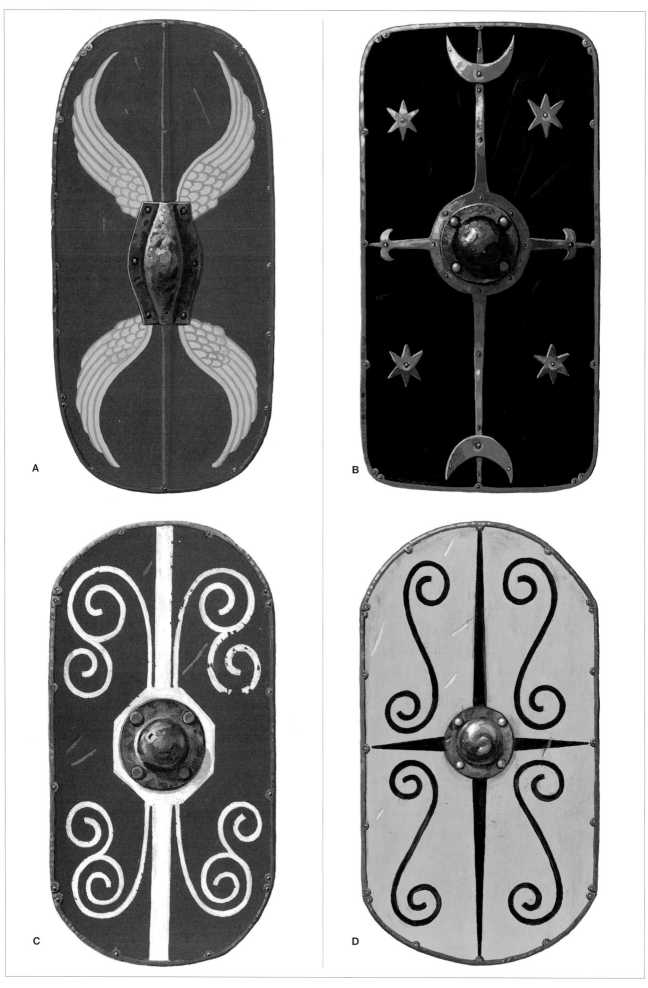

A

B

C

D

E

F

G

H

connection.

It has become traditional to depict legionary shields in both artistic and actual reconstructions in a red colour, indeed the rectangular Dura shield was this colour. However other colours may have been used as well. During the Civil Wars of the First century AD, two Praetorian soldiers passed through enemy lines to disable a catapult by the simple means of using shields taken off dead soldiers from the other side. Obviously it was possible to identify different units by their distinctive shield emblems and this could have been

Previous pages.
As well as the curved rectangular shield, the Romans used a number of different shield designs. These reconstructions are based on actual surviving examples or shield covers which help to give dimensions. With the exception of (g) all the colour schemes are hypothetical but are inspired by shield colours on contemporary mosaics and frescos. The straight sided shields with rounded upper and lower edges are only known from shield cover finds they are not depicted anywhere in Roman art. As yet no positive archaeological evidence has been recovered for the hexagonal shields that are sometimes shown on sculptures. A: Fayum; B: Doncaster; C: Valkenburg; D: Caerleon; E: Castleford; F: Valkenburg; G: Dura-Europos; H: Dura-Europos.

Two views of a hand held *manuballista* reconstructed by Bernard Jacobs of the *Ermine Street Guard*. The *manuballista* was described by the ancient historian Heron and was an iron framed torsion crossbow of the type which was cocked by pressing down on a crescent shaped pad at the back with the stomach. Earlier versions of these machines were nicknamed 'belly bows'. The iron frame at the front holds rope bundles which provide the motive power for firing the projectiles. Similar but slightly larger iron framed catapults appear on Trajan's Column.

Complete example of a catapult bolt with wooden shaft discovered at Dura-Europos.

further assisted if a variety of colours were used. This could be supported by two shields recently discovered at Masada, one was red the other blue. On a mosaic from Zliten in Algeria depicting a gladiatorial event, a number of rectangular shields are shown, some of these are in red with white and black patterns, others in yellow with white and black patterns. While this is not a military scene it may be suggestive of contemporary colour schemes.

Many of the shield designs featuring astrological symbols such as stars and moons could imply they were painted on a black or dark blue background. Black was a common colour in Roman wall paintings in particular as a background to light green foliage, a combination which could also have appeared on many shield designs with leaf patterns. Apart from the rectangular shield, two oval shields form Dura also had a red background. All three featured highly complex motifs with mythological figures and animals. The majority of the other Dura shields had pink backgrounds, while another had a grey green base with a full length figure of a warrior god. Elaborate

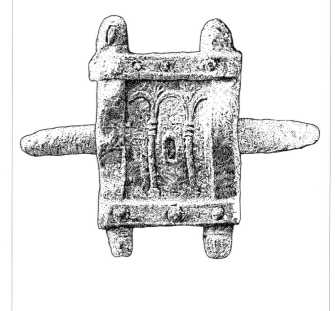

Front view of a bolt shooting artillery machine showing a decorated plate, on the tombstone of C. Vedennius Moderatus in Rome. The plate is similar to the one found at Cremona.

Detail of the embossed *Phalerae* and leather harness worn by the reconstructed Centurion of the *Ermine Street Guard*.

Detail of neck *torques* and reconstructed method of attachment looped onto fabric hung around the back of the neck.

shields such as these are often labelled parade shields, display copies for shield makers, or even antiques. Even the backs of shields could be painted. One of the Dura shields has heart and rosette motifs on the reverse painted on a dark blue background. Experiments using authentic pigments and tempera medium to paint replica shields have not been entirely successful. The paint is easily scratched or flakes and even if only slightly wet rubs off on to tunics, this would imply a stronger medium was used, perhaps casein, as suggested after the original study of the Dura shields.

Artillery

Bolt shooters *catapultae* and stone throwers *ballistae* were the two main types or artillery in use in Roman times. A legion probably had one stone thrower for each of the ten Cohorts and approximately 60 bolt shooters, one per century. Roman artillery was inherited from Greek and Macedonian technology. Both these types of machine operated on the torsion principle, with wooden arms in twisted skeins of sinew or hair. Small bolt shooting machines were probably

no more than two metres high, but machines that were capable of throwing stones weighing over 45 kilos were obviously much larger. It was conceivably a stone from one of these machines that took the head off a defender of Jerusalem and, according to Josephus the Jewish historian, carried it for three furlongs.

Artillery was mainly used during sieges, the smaller machines however could be used on board ships or mounted on carts where they could act as a form of mobile artillery, in addition some developments did take place during the Roman period. The wooden frames of the smaller bolt shooters appear to have been replaced in metal. A shield from the front of a machine was found at the battle site of Cremona, it was originally believed to be the lid of a legionary pay chest. There appears to be no firm evidence that artillery was ever used by the Auxilia.

Military Decorations (*Dona Militaria*)

The system of awards in the Roman Army was quite a complex one, dependent on rank and status as well as merit, and a wide range of decorations was available.

Some of the reconstructed camp equipment used during the march across the Alps by Marcus Junkelmann's Augustan period legionaries. A *patera* metal flask and rotary quern stone for grinding grain can be seen.

These included a number of crowns such as the *Corona Civica* (Civic Crown) awarded for saving a fellow citizens life, spears and flags. But the most familiar are the *Torques* (neck rings) *Armillae* (armlets) and *Phalerae* (discs). Some of these awards arose out of the practice of looting the bodies of fallen enemies, in particularly the Celts. The most obvious example of this is the Celtic neck torque which was adopted by the Romans but instead worn around the neck in a set of two probably attached by a strap.

Although normally in civilian contexts considered an effeminate practice, *Armillae* sometimes in the form of snakes were also worn by soldiers and again this seems to have been adopted from the Celts. Many sculptures of Centurions show them wearing *Phalerae*

Eight man *contuburnia* tent reconstructed by Bill Mayes and Tim Haines of the *Ermine Street Guard*. The stitching methods employed by the Romans ensured that the seams overlapped and were waterproof . When not in use the tent would be carried by a mule which was allocated to each unit of eight men.

A legionary loads up a pack mule on Trajan's Column. A long handled cooking utensil *Patera* can clearly be seen.

Four wheeled cart with shields and arms from the column of Marcus Aurelius.

and they have become firmly associated with this rank although they were not exclusively awarded to Centurions. *Phalerae* were worn in sets of five, seven or nine and attached to a leather harness worn around the body, while some individual *Phalerae* were based on classical or mythological subjects in the form of duties or creatures, many were simple circular or rosette motifs. The only complete surviving set of *Phalerae* was found a Lauersfort in Germany in 1858.

Auxiliaries rarely received individual awards for bravery, instead the system developed whereby decorations were awarded to the entire unit which was then commemorated in the unit title, *Torquata* for example. The granting of Citizenship was another way of rewarding Auxiliaries either individually or to the unit as a whole. Again this would be recorded in the unit's title. One such unit serving in Britain was the elite cavalry regiment nominally one thousand strong, named after T. Pomponius Petra, probably the original commander, and raised in Gaul during the reign of Augustus. The unit received Roman citizenship from the Emperor Domitianus and was awarded two *Torques* hence its full title was ALA

AUGUSTA GALLORUM PETRIANA MILLIARIA CIVIUM ROMANORUM BIS TORQUATA.

Ownership and Development of Equipment

When a recruit joined the army he was provided with weapons, uniform and equipment for which money was deducted from his pay at source. Soldiers could use their equipment as collateral for loans or it could even be used in lieu of money by provincial governors to help finance rebellions. Soldiers may also have offered part of their equipment like swords and helmets as ritual deposits, which may account for the high proportion of equipment found in rivers or near water. As it would of course have been an offence to be without equipment, the soldier would have had to have made provision for this beforehand. Equipment or clothing could be provided as gifts, sometimes from the soldiers family and friends or in rare cases by a military commander. Apparently the cost deducted for equipment did not match that of inflation and the problem of soldiers selling their equipment and keeping the profit became so serious it required Imperial intervention.

A legionary collecting forage on Trajan's Column.

Transporting horses by boat in a scene from Trajan's Column.

When soldiers were discharged, their weapons and equipment were probably bought back by the unit. In the event of the soldier's death before discharge, their wills would stipulate where the returned money was to be sent. There is some evidence that soldiers kept their weapons after service, either selling them on the open market, although these may have been privately owned, or in extreme cases being buried with them.

Roman equipment and armour underwent many changes even during the period covered by this book. This was due to many circumstances, some not always understood. Movement of units or individuals helped to spread new ideas or fashions while other troops remained static and their influence was therefore localised. Equipment would alter as a result of battlefield modifications, the adding of cross pieces on helmets for instance, or on the whims of powerful individuals. Also interaction with the enemies of Rome meant that the frontier armies were constantly faced with new innovations and weapons, many of which ultimately found their way into the Imperial armies.

Field Equipment

The Roman army used a variety of tools and field equipment many of which remained familiar until modern times. Those most readily associated with the army are the *dolabra*, palisade stakes, turf cutter and the *groma*.

The dolabra was a multipurpose tool combining a cutting blade which on Trajan's Column is shown being used to fell trees and a crooked pick end for breaking up earth. Recent experiments with a *dolabra* found it superior to a modern pick and it was even

Pick axe *dolabra*.

possible to cut turf with the axe-head. A sheath made from copper alloy was used to cover the blade when not in use which in true Roman fashion was often decorated, sometimes with pendants. The Roman general Corbulo certainly believed that more battles were won with the *dolabra* rather than the *gladius*.

Pointed oak stakes with a narrow 'hand-grip' found on a couple of sites are usually referred to as palisade stakes. The implication being that they were knocked into the turf and lashed together at the grip to form a barrier around temporary camps. Opinion has been divided over the correct identification of these stakes, historians calling them either *Valli* or *Pilum Murale*, although the latter references seemed better suited to a throwing weapon. Over seventy of these stakes were found at Oberaden, some of them inscribed with a Centurial mark suggesting they did not belong to individual soldiers. The Oberaden stakes show no signs of being hammered into the ground implying they may originally have been used as *chevaux-de-frise*.

Due to their resemblance to the modern garden tool used for edging lawns, the anchor shaped blades discovered on many Roman sites have been labelled turf cutters. There is, however, no positive support for this identification. Indeed practical experiments with reconstructed Turf Cutters have almost without exception failed to successfully carry out the task for which they were supposedly intended. As mentioned earlier the *dolabra*, is quite useful in cutting turf, so is a spade. It would therefore appear to be an unnecessary encumbrance for soldiers to carry a tool the sole function of which could more easily be performed by other tools readily to hand. In fact the Turf Cutters resemble two other fairly modern implements. The smaller type is very similar to leather cutting knives, while the larger version is paralleled by a bark stripper. Both of these uses would of course have been utilised in the Roman army which was heavily reliant on leather goods. A leather cutter would therefore need no explanation while a source of tannin for curing leather was from bark.

For the measurement of right angles, Roman *mensores*, surveyors, used a *Groma*. The *Groma* was an instrument with four arms on a cross frame at ninety degrees to each other and suspended from each arm was a plumb line. The frame was positioned on a pole off centre so the surveyor could view through the plumb lines at different angles. Even with eight lead weights, the lines can move about in high winds, which may account for some fort plans that are out of alignment. Part of a *Groma* was found at the fort at Pfunz in Germany but a better preserved example was excavated at Pompeii. Surveyors would also use measuring poles ten Roman feet long called *Decempedae*. Any investigation of Roman forts often reveals dimensions that are simply multiples of five or ten Roman feet. The reconstructed *Groma* produced by the *Ermine Street Guard* always attracts comment and the public are surprised to discover that it is in fact a surveying instrument and not a Roman helicopter!

Each Century in a Legion or Cohort was subdivided into ten eight-man units called a *Contuburnia*. In permanent forts, the eight men shared a barrack room which in size had originated from the tent used in marching camps. A modern reconstruction of a tent produced by the *Ermine Street Guard* required seventy seven goatskins, giving an idea of the amount of leather that would be required to equip even a single legion with tents. Even at full capacity there is soom room available for the storage of equipment. Seams on Roman tents consisted of reinforcing strips that were whip-stitched to produce waterproof stitches with no visible signs of stitching. The reconstructed tent weighs 44 (kg.) but this can increase by as much as 8 (kg.) with absorption or rainwater.

Bibliography

List of Abbreviations

Ant. J. = Antiquaries Journal.

A.N.R.W. = Aufstieg und Niedergang der Römischen Welt.

B.J. = Bonner Jahrbücher.

Brit. = Britannia.

C.S.I.R. = Corpus Signorum Imperii Romani.

J.R.M.E.S. = Journal of Roman Military Equipment Studies.

J.R.S. = Journal of Roman Studies.

P.E.Q. = Palestine Exploration Quarterly.

S.M.R. III = Studien zu den Militärgrenzen Roms III: 13. Internationaler Limeskongress Stuttgart (1986).

Alföldy. G., *Geschichte des Römischen Heeres*, Amsterdam (1987).

Allason-Jones. L. and Bishop. M. C., *Excavations at Roman Corbridge: The Hoard*, London (1988).

Alston. R., *Soldier and Society in Roman Egypt*, London (1995).

Amy. R., Picard. G. -Ch., Hatt. J. -J. Dural, P. -M., Picard, Ch. and Piganiol. A., *L'arc d' Orange*, Gallia, Suppl. 15 (1962).

Anderson. A. S., *Roman Military Tombstones*, Princes Risborough (1984).

Baatz. D. and Herrmann. F. R., *Die Römer in Hessen*, Stuttgart (1982).

Baatz. D., *Ein Katapult der Legio IV Macedonica aus Cremona*, M.D.A.I. (R) 87 (1980).

Baatz. D., *Recent Finds of Ancient Artillery*, Brit. 9 (1978).

Balty. J. C. H., *Apamea in Syria in the Second and Third Centuries AD*, J.R.S. (1988).

Balty. J., *Guide d' Apamee*, Bruxelles (1981).

Bandinelli. R. B., *Leptis Magna*, Italy (1964).

Barker. P., *The Armies and Enemies of Imperial Rome*, Worthing (1981).

Becatti. G., *Colonna di Marco Aurelio*, Milano (1957).

Bechert.T. and Willems. W. J. H., *Die Römische Reichsgrenze zwischen Mosel und Nordsee-Küste*, Stuttgart (1995).

Bellet. M. E., *Orange Antique: Guides Archéologiques de la France* (1991).

Bellinger. A., Brown. F., Perkins. A. and Welles. C., *The Excavations at Dura-Europos*. Final Report VIII. Part 1, New Haven (1956).

Bennett. J., *A Roman Helmet in the Dominican Republic*, in Van Driel-Murray. C. ed. (1989)

Birley. A., *Septimius Severus the African Emperor*, London (1971).

Birley. E., *Roman Army Papers*, Amsterdam (1988).

Birley. E., *Septimius Severus and the Roman Army*, Epigraphische Studien 8 (1969).

Birley. E., Dobson. B. and Jarrett. M. G. eds., *Roman Frontier Studies*, 1969: *Eighth International Congress of Limesforschung*. Cardiff (1974).

Birley. R., *Garrison Life on the Roman Frontier*, Greenhead (1994).

Birley. R., *Vindolanda: A Roman frontier post on Hadrians Wall*, London (1977).

Birley. R., *Vindolanda*, Greenhead (1995).

Bishop M.C., *The Military Fabrica and the Production of Arms in the Early Principate*, in Bishop. M. C. ed. (1985).

Bishop. M. C. ed., *Roman Military Equipment, proceedings of a seminar*, Sheffield (1983).

Bishop. M. C. and Coulston. J. C., *Roman Military Equipment*, Princes Risbourough (1989).

Bishop. M. C., *Aketon, Thoracomachus, and Lorica Segmentata*, Exercitus 3.1 (1995).

Bishop. M. C., *Cavalry Equipment of the Roman Army in the First Century AD*, in Coulston. J. C. ed. (1986).

Bishop. M. C., *Legio V Alaudae and the Crested Lark*, J.R.M.E.S. 1 (1990).

Bishop. M. C., *The Camomile Street Soldier reconsidered*, London and Middlesex (1983).

Bishop. M. C. ed, *The Production and Distribution of Roman Military Equipment*. Second proceedings of the Roman Military Equipment Research Seminar. B.A.R. Int. Ser. 275, Oxford (1985).

Bishop. M. C., *Cavalry Equipment of the Roman Army in the 1ˢᵗ Century AD*, in Coulston J. C. ed. (1988).

Bodley. A. and Garlick. M., *The Construction and Use of Roman Cavalry Equipment*, Exercitus 2.10 (1994).

Bogaers. J. E. ed., *Studien zu den Militärgrenzen Roms II.*, Köln (1977).

Boon. G. C., *A Trulleus from Caerleon with a Stamp of The First Cavalry Regiment of Thracians*, Ant. J. (1984).

Boon. G. C., *Isca: The Roman Legionary Fortress at Caerleon*, Cardiff (1972).

Boube-Piccot. C., *Les bronze antiques du Maroc*, Vol. 4 Paris (1994).

Bounni. A. and Al-Asád. K., *Palmyre, Histoire, Monuments et Musee*, Damas (1987).

Bowersock. G., *Roman Arabia*, Harvard (1983).

Bowman. A. K. and Adams. J. N., *Two letters from Vindolanda*, Brit. 21 (1990).

Bowman. A. K. and Thomas. J. D., *Vindolanda. The Latin Writing Tablets*, London (1983).

Bowman. A. K. and Thomas. J. D., *Vindolanda (1985) The New Latin Writing Tablets*, J.R.S. 76 (1985).

Bowsher. J. M. C., *The Nabatean Army*, in French. D. H. and Lightfoot. C. S. eds. (1989).

Bowsher. J., *The Frontier post of Medain Saleh*, in Freeman. P. and Kennedy. D. eds. (1966).

Brailsford. J. W., *Hod Hill 1: Antiquities from Hod Hill in the Durden Collection*, London (1962).

Breeze. D. J. and Dobson. B., *Hadrians Wall*, London (1987).

Breeze. D. J. and Dobson. B., *Roman Officers and Frontiers*, Stuttgart (1993).

Breeze. D. J., Close-Brooks. J. and Ritchie. J., *Soldiers Burials at Camelon, Stirlingshire*, Brit. 7 (1976).

Breeze. D. J., *The Career Structure below the Centurionate during the Principate*. A.N.R.W. II (1974).

Breeze. D. J., *The organisation of the Career Structure of the Immunes and Principalis of the Roman Army*, B. J. (1974).

Bishop. M. C., *The Corbridge Hoard*, Exercitus 2.3. (1987).

Brunsting. H. and Steures. D. C., *The Nijmegen Helmet and an unusual Umbo*, Arma 3 (1991).

Buckland. P., *A First Century Shield from Doncaster, Yorkshire*, Brit. 9 (1978).

Burger. A. and Furep. F., *Die Römischen Inschriften Ungarns (4)*, Bonn (1984).

Brewer. R., *Caerleon - Isca*, Cardiff (1987).

Cambell. B., *The Roman Army 31 BC - AD 337. A Source Book*, London (1994).

Campbell. D. B., *Auxiliary Artillery revisited*, B.J. 186 (1986).

Cansdale. G. S., *Animals from Bible Lands*, Exeter (1970).

Carrick. P., *Painting a Roman Shield*, Arbeia Journal (1993).

Carter. J., *The Battle of Actium*, London (1970).

Cheesman. G. L., *The Auxilia of the Roman Imperial Army*, Oxford (1914).

Cichorius. C., *Die Reliefs der Traianssäule*, Berlin (1896-1900).

Connolly. P., *Experiments with the Roman Saddle*, Exercitus 2.5. (1988).

Connolly. P., *A note on the origins of the Imperial Gallic helmet*, in Van Driel-Murray. C. ed. (1989).

Connolly. P., *Greece and Rome at War*, London (1981).

Connolly. P., *Living in the Time of Jesus of Nazareth*, Oxford (1983).

Connolly. P., *The fastening of the Gladius to the belt in the early Empire*, Arma 3 (1991).

Connolly. P., *The Roman Army*, London (1975).

Connolly. P., *The Roman fighting technique deduced from armour and weaponry*, in Maxfield. V. A. and Dobson. M. J. eds. (1991).

Connolly. P., *The Roman fort*, Oxford (1991).

Connolly. P., *The Roman Saddle*, in Dawson. M. ed. (1987).

Connolly. P., *Tiberius Claudius Maximus: the Cavalryman*, Oxford (1988).

Connolly. P., *Tiberius Claudius Maximus: the Legionary*, Oxford (1988).

Constable. C., *The Ermine Street Guard*, Dossiers de l' Archéologie 86 (1984).

Constable. C., *Reconstruction of an Imaginifer's Uniform*, Exercitus 2.4. (1988).

Cormac. J. M. R., *Epitaph of a Legionary of the Legio XVI Flavia Firma from Macedonia*, J.R.S. 31 (1941).

Couissin. P., *Les Armes Romaines*, Paris (1926).

Coulston. J. C. ed., *Military Equipment and the Identity of Roman Soldiers*. Proceedings of the Fourth Roman Military Equipment Conference. B.A.R. Int. Ser. 394, Oxford (1988).

Coulston. J. C. N., *Later Roman Armour 3ʳᵈ - 6ᵗʰ Centuries AD*, J.R.M.E.S. 1 (1990).

Coulston. J. C. N., *The Draco Standard*, J.R.M.E.S. 2 (1991).

Coulston. J. C., *Roman Archery Equipment*, in Bishop. M. C. ed. (1985).

Coulston. J. C., *Roman Military Equipment on 3ʳᵈ Century AD tombstones*, in Dawson. M. ed. (1987).

Coulston. J. C., *Three Legionaries at Croy Hill*, in Coulston J. C. ed. (1988).

Craddock. P. T., Lang. J. and Painte. K. S., *Roman Horse Trappings from Fremington Hagg, Reeth, Yorkshire*, Brit. Mus. Qtly. (1973).

Croom. A. T., *Quinta's Wooden Practice Sword*, Arbeia Journal (1992).

Croom. A. T., *The Painted Vexillum and Shields*, Arbeia Journal (1994).

Croom. A. T., *The Reconstruction of a Roman Vexillum*, Arbeia Journal (1993).

C. S. I. R., *C. S. I. R. Österreich* II, Wien (1994).

C. S. I. R., *C. S. I. R. Deutschland* II.*5 Germania Superior*, Mainz (1992).

C. S. I. R., *C. S. I. R. Deutschland* I *Raetia-Noricum*, Bonn (1973).

C. S. I. R., *C. S. I. R. Deutschland* III *Germania Inferior*, Bonn (1998).

Cüppers. H., *Die Römer in Rheinland-Pfalz*, Stuttgart (1990).

Curle. J., *A Roman frontier post and its people. The fort of Newstead in the parish of Melrose*, Glasgow (1911)

Czysz. W., *Wiesbaden in der Römerzeit*, Stuttgart (1994).

Dabrowa. E., *Dromedarii in the Roman Army*, in Maxfield. V. A. and Dobson. M. J. eds. (1981).

Daniels. C., *A hoard of Iron and other materials from Corbridge*, A. A. 46 (1968).

Darde. D. G. and Lassalle. V., *Nimes Antique: Guides Archéologiques De la France* (1993).

Davies. J. L., *Roman Arrowheads from Dinorben and the sagittarii of the Roman Army*, Brit. 8 (1977).

Davies. R. W., *Cohors I Numidarum and a Roman Military document from Egypt.*

Davies. R. W., *Service in the Roman Army*, Edinburgh (1989).

Dawson. M. ed., *Roman Military Equipment: the Accoutrements of war. Proceedings of the third Roman Military Equipment Research Seminar*, B.A.R. Int. Ser. 336, Oxford (1987).

Dawson. M., *A review of the equipment of the Roman army of Dacia*, in Van Driel-Murray. C. ed. (1989).

Dawson. M., *Roman Military Equipment, the Accoutrements of War*, in Dawson. M. ed. (1987).

De Villard. U. M., *The Temple of the Imperial Cult at Luxor*, Archaeologia 95 (1953).

Devijver. H., *Equestrian Officers of the Roman Army 1*, Amsterdam (1989).

Devijver. H., *Equestrian Officers of the Roman Army 2*, Amsterdam (1992).

Dilke. O. A. W., *The Roman Land Surveyors. An introduction to the Agrimensores*, Newton Abbot (1971).

Dixon. K. R. *Dolphin Scabbard runners*, J.R.M.E.S. 1 (1990).

Dixon. K. R. and Southern. P., *The Roman Cavalry*, London (1992).

Dobson. B. and Mann. J. C., *The Roman Army in Britain and Britons in the Roman Army*, Brit. 4 (1973).

Dobson. B., *The Empire* in *Warfare in the Ancient World*, Hackett. J. ed., London (1989).

Dodgeon. M. H. and Lieu. S. N. C., *The Roman Eastern Frontier and Persian Wars AD 226-363*, London (1991).

Doxiadis. E., *The Mysterious Fayum Portraits: Faces from Ancient Egypt*, London (1972).

Eadie. J., *The Development of Roman Mailed Cavalry*, J.R.S. 57 (1967).

Elbe. J. Von., *The Romans in Cologne and Lower Germany*, Bonn (1995).

Esperandieu. E., *Bas reliefs de la Gaule Romaine*, Paris (1907).

Filtzinger. P., *Limesmuseum Aalen*, Stuttgart (1983).

Fink. R. O., *Roman Military records on Papyrus*, Cleveland (1971).

Florescu. F. B., *Das Siegesdenkmal von Adamklissi Tropaeum Traiani*, Bucharest (1965).

Forestier. A., *The Roman Soldier*, London (1928).

Freeman P. and Kennedy. D. eds., *The Defence of the Roman and Byzantine East: proceedings of a colloquium*, B.A.R. Int. Ser. 297, Oxford (1986).

French D. H. and Lightfoot. C. S. eds., *The Eastern Frontier of the Roman Empire: proceedings of a Colloquium*, B.A.R. Int. Ser. 553, Oxford (1989).

French. E., *Nabatean Warrior Saddles*, P.E.Q. 120 (1988).

Frere. S. S. and St Joseph. J. K., *The Roman fortress at Longthorpe*, Brit. 5 (1974)

Fuentes. N., *The Mule of a Soldier*, J.R.M.E.S. 2 (1991).

Fuentes. N., *The Roman Military Tunic*, in Dawson. M. ed. (1987).

Fuentes. N., *The Legionary Scutum*, Exercitus 1.1. (1980).

Gablemann. H., *Die Typen der Römischen Grabstelen am Rhein*, B.J. 172 (1972).

Gablemann. H., *Römische Grabmonumente mit Reiterkampfszenen im Rheingebiet*, B.J. 173 (1973).

Garbsch. J., *Römische Paraderüstungen*, München (1978).

Garlick. M., *Reconstruction and use of a Lorica Hamata*, Exercitus 1.1. (1980).

Garlick. M., *Reconstruction of a Cornu*, Exercitus 2.1. (1986).

Garlick. M., *Reconstructing a pair of Greaves*, Exercitus 1.9. (1984).

Gerhartl-Witteüeen, A. M. and Hubrecht. A. V. M., *Survey of Swords and Daggers in the Provincial Museum G.M. Kam, Nijmegen*, J.R.M.E.S. (1990).

Germania 74 (1996).

Gilliam. J. F., *Roman Army Papers*, Amsterdam (1986).

Gilliam. J. F., *The Deposita of an Auxiliary Soldier*, B.J. 167 (1967).

Gore. R., *The Dead do tell tales at Vesuvius*, National Geographic 165:5 (1984).

Grant. M., *Gladiators*, New York (1995).

Grew. F. and Griffiths. N., *The Pre-Flavian military belt: the evidence from Britain*, Archaeologia 109 (1991).

Greep. S., *Ribbed Gladius Handles of the First Century AD*, Exercitus 1.9. (1984).

Griffiths. W. B. and Carrick. P., *Reconstructing Roman Slings*, Arbcia Journal (1994).

Griffiths. W. B. and Sim. D., *Experiments with Replica Roman Javelins*, Arbeia Journal (1993).

Griffiths. W. B., *The Hand Thrown Stone*, Arbeia Journal (1992).

Griffiths. W. B., *The Sling and its Place in the Roman Imperial Army*, in Van Driel-Murray. C. ed. (1989).

Grimal. P., *The Civilization of Rome*, London (1983).

Groenman-Van Waateringe. W, *Romeins lederwerk uit Valkenburg*, Groningen (1967).

Grünewald. M., *Die Römer in Worms*, Stuttgart (1986).

Günther. R. and Köpstien., *Die Römer an Rhein und Donau*, Köln (1978).

Haines. C., *A short history of the Ermine Street Guard*, Exercitus 1 (1980).

Hald. M., *The Textiles of Ancient Denmark*, Copenhagen (1950)

Hanson. W. S. and Keppie. L., eds. *Roman Frontier Studies 1979. Papers presented to the 12th International Congress*. B.A.R. Int. Ser. 71, Oxford (1980).

Hassall. M. W. C., *Batavians and the Roman Conquest of Britain*, Brit. 1 (1970).

Hassall. M. W. C., *Roman harness fittings from Canterbury*, Ant. J. 60 (1980).

Hazell. P., *The pedite gladius*, Ant. J. 61 (1982).

Henig. M. ed., *A Handbook of Roman Art*, Oxford (1983).

Holder. P., *Studies in the Auxilia of the Roman Army*, B.A.R. Int. Ser. 70, Oxford (1980).

Holder. P., *The Roman Army in Britain*, London (1982).

Horn. H. G., *Die Römer in Nordrhein-Westfalen*, Stuttgart (1987).

Horn. H. G., *Römishe Steindenkmäler 3*, Bonn (1981).

Hyland. A., *Training the Roman Cavalry*, Gloucester (1993).

Hyland. A., *Equus. The Horse in the Roman World*, London (1990).

James. S., *Evidence from Dura Europos for the origins of late Roman helmets*, Syria 63 (1986).

Jenkins. I. D., *A group of silvered-bronze horse trappings from Xanten*, Brit. 16 (1985).

Johnson. A., *Roman Forts of the 1st and 2nd Centuries AD in Britain and the German Provinces*, London (1983).

Junkelmann. M., *Die Legionen des Augustus*, Mainz (1986).

Junkelmann. M., *Die Reiter Roms (3 Vols)*, Mainz (1992).

Junkelmann. M., *Reiter wie Statuen aus Erz*, Mainz (1996).

Kalavrezor-Maxeiner. I., *The Imperial Chamber at Luxor*, Dumbarton Oaks Papers 29 (1975).

Kalee. C. A., *Roman Helmets and other militaria from Vechten*, in Van Driel-Murray. C. ed. (1989).

Kennedy D. L., *Some observations on the Praetorian Guard*, Ancient Society 9 (1978).

Kennedy. D. L. and Riley. D., *Romes Desert Frontier from the Air*, London (1990).

Kennedy. D. L., *The Military Contribution of Syria to the Roman Imperial Army*, in French. D. H. and Lightfoot. C. S. eds. (1989).

Kennedy. D., *The Ala I and Cohors I Britannica*, Britt. 8 (1977).

Keppie. L. *The making of the Roman Army from Republic to Empire*, London (1984).

Keppie. L., *Understanding Roman Inscriptions*, London (1991).

Klee. M., *Der Limes zwischen Rhein und Main*, Stuttgart (1989).

Klumbach. H., *Römische Helme aus Niedergermanien*, Köln (1974).

Klumbach. H., *Spätrömische Gardehelme*, München (1973).

Knight. J., *Caerleon Roman Fortress*, Cardiff (1988)

Kocsis. L., *Ein neugefunder Römischer Helm aus dem Legionslager von Aquincum*, S.M.R. III.

Kos. M. S., *A Latin epitaph of a Roman Legionary from Corinth*, J.R.S. 68 (1978).

Kraeling. C. H., *The Excavations at Dura-Europos Final Report VIII. 1: The Synagogue*, New Haven (1956).

Kreckovič. E., *Military equipment on the territory of Slovakia*, J.R.M.E.S. 5 (1994).

Kruger. M. L., *C. S. I. R. Österreich (Band 1) Carnuntum*, Wien (1970).

Kunnen. H. P., *Der Sarazenensattel: zu den Voraussetzungen der Sarazeneneinfälle am Limes Arabiae*, in Maxfield. V. A. and Dobson. M. J. eds. (1991).

Lang. J., *A Study of the Metallography of some Roman Swords*, Brit. 19 (1988).

Le Bohec. Y., *L'armée romaine sous le haut-empire*, Paris (1989).

Leander Touati. A. M., *The Great Trajanic Frieze, the Study of a Monument and of the Mechanics of Message Transmission in Roman Art*, Stockholm (1987).

Lerat. L., *Besançon Antique: Guides Archéologiques De la France* (1990).

Lepper. F. and Frere. S., *Trajans Column*, Gloucester (1988)

Leva. C. and Plumier. J., *La XXe Légion revit*, Dossiers de l' Archéologie (1984).

Lewis. N. and Reinhold. M., *Roman Civilization. Source Book 11. The Empire*, New York (1955).

Liversidge. M. and Edwards. C. eds., *Imagining Rome. British Artists and Rome in the Nineteenth Century*, London (1996).

Lloyd-Morgan. G.*Professor Robert Newstead and Finds of Roman Military Metalwork from Chester*, in Dawson. M. ed. (1987).

Marchant. D., *Roman Weapons in Great Britain, a Case Study: Spearheads, problems in dating and typology*, J.R.M.E.S. 1 (1990).

Marsden. E. W., *Greek and Roman Artillery*, Oxford (1971).

Marsden. P., *Roman London*, London (1980).

Martin. M., *Römermuseum und Römerhaus Augst*, Augst (1981).

Massey. D., *Roman Archery Tested*, Military Illustrated. 74 (1994).

Mattingly. D., *Tripolitania*, London (1995).

Maxfield. V., *Roman Military Torques*, Exercitus 2.4. (1988).

Maxfield. V., *The Military Decorations of the Roman Army*, London (1981).

Maxfield. V. A. and Dobson. M. J. eds., *Roman Frontier Studies, 1989. Proceedings of the 15th International Congress of Roman Frontier Studies*, Exeter (1991).

Maxfield. V. A., *Pre-Flavian forts and their garrisons*, Brit. 17 (1986)

Mayes. B., *The Reconstruction of a Leather Tent*, Exercitus 2.10 (1994).

Menen. A., *Cities in the Sand*, Norwich (1972).

Michalowski. K., *Palmyre, Fouilles Polonaises (1960)*, Warsaw (1962).

Millar. F., *The Roman Near East 31 BC - AD 337*, Harvard (1993).

Milner. N. P., *Vegetius Epitome of Military Science*, Liverpool (1993).

Mirković. M., *Beneficiarii Consularis and the New Outpost in Sirmium*, in Maxfield. V. A. and Dobson. M. J. eds. (1991).

Morel. J., *The Roman Dagger and Belt Fittings from Velsen, Netherlands*, Exercitus 2.6. (1989).

Morgan. L., *Reconstruction of a Groma*, Exercitus 1.2. (1980).

Nicolle. D., *Rome's Enemies (5) The Desert Frontier*, London (1991).

Nicolle. D., *Sassanian Armies*, Stockport (1996).

Peterson. D., *The Roman Legions Recreated in Colour Photographs*, London (1992).

Oldenstein. J., *Two Roman Helmets from Eich, Alzey-Worms district*, J.R.M.E.S. 1 (1990).

Peddie. J. *The Roman War Machine*, Gloucester (1994).

Pfahl. S. and Reuter. M., *Waffen aus Römischen Einzelsiedlungen rechts des Rheins*, Germania 74 (1996).

Phillips. E. D., *The Royal Hordes Nomad People of the Steppes*, London (1965)

Poulter. A. G., *Certain Doubts and Doubtful Conclusions. The Lorica Segmentata from Newstead and the Antonine Garrison*, in Coulston. J. C. ed. (1988).

Price. P., *An interesting find of Lorica Plumata from the Roman Fortress at Usk*, in Bishop. M. C. (1983).

Protase. D., *Das Römerlager von Brincovenesti*, in Bogaers. J. E. ed. (1977).

Rabiesen. E., *La production d'équipment de Cavalerie au 1er s après J-C à Alesia*, in J.R.M.E.S. 1 (1990).

Rankov. B., *The Praetorian Guard*, London (1994).

Richmond. I. A., *Trajan's Army on Trajan's Column*, London (1982).

Rieche. A. and Schalles. H. J., *Colonia Ulpia Traiana: Arbeit, Handwerk und Berufe in der Römischen Stadt*, Bonn (1987).

Robinson. H. R. and Embleton. R., *The Armour of the Roman Legions*, Newcastle.

Robinson. H. R., *Problems in reconstructing Roman Armour*, in Birley. E. Dobson. B. and Jarrett. M. G. eds. (1974).

Robinson. H. R., *The Armour of Imperial Rome*, London (1975).

Robinson. H. R., *The Origins of some 1st Century Legionary helmets*, in Bogaers. J. E. ed. (1977).

Robinson. H. R., *What the soldiers wore on Hadrians Wall*, Newcastle (1979).

Robinson. R., *Problems in reconstructing Roman armour*, B. J. 172 (1972).

Rostovtzeff. M., Bellinger. A., Brown. F., Tuil. M. P. and Welles. C. eds., *The Excavations at Dura Europos. Final Report IV Part 11*, New Haven (1945).

Rostovtzeff. M., et al, *Excavations at Dura-Europos. Preliminary Report of The Sixth Season of Work 1932-1933*, New Haven (1936).

Rostovtzeff. M., *The Excavations at Dura-Europos. Preliminary Report*, New Haven (1930).

Ryberg. I. S., *Panel Reliefs of Marcus Aurelius*, New York (1967).

Saddington. D. B., *The Development of the Roman Auxiliary Forces from Augustus to Trajan*, A.N.R.W. II, 3, Berlin (1975).

Salama. P., *Masque-de Parade et casque d' Ain Grimidi*, in S.M.R. III (1986).

Saluiat. F., *Glanum: Guides Archéologiques de la France* (1990).

Schatzmann. I., *Artillery in Judaea from Hasmonaean to Roman Times*, in French. D. H. and Lightfoot. C. S. eds. (1989).

Schleirmacher. M., *Römische Reitergrabsteine, die kaiserzeitlichen Reliefs des triumphierenden Reiters*, Bonn (1984).

Schmidt-Colinets. A., *Das Tempelgrab Nr 36 in Palmyra*, Mainz (1992).

Schülter. W. and Berger. E., *Kalkriese Römer im Osnabrücker Land*, Rasch (1993).

Schülter. W., *Archäologische Zeugnisse zur Varusschlacht*, Germania 70 (1992).

Scott. I. R., *First Century Military daggers and the manufacture and supply of weapons for the Roman Army*, in Bishop. M. C. ed. (1985).

Selzer. W., *Römische Steindenkmäler. Mainz in Römischer Zeit*, Mainz (1988).

Shaw. T., *Roman Cloaks*, Exercitus 1.4 (1982) and 1.5 (1982).

Shore. A. F., *Portrait Painting from Roman Egypt*, London (1972).

Shortt. H., *A provincial Roman Spur from Longstock, Hants, and other Spurs from Roman Britain*, Ant. J. 39 (1959).

Sim. D., *Manufacture of Javelin Heads*, Arbeia Journal (1993).

Simkins. M., *The Roman Army from Caesar to Trajan*, London (1974).

Simkins. M., *The Roman Army from Caesar to Trajan.* (Revised Edition), London (1984).

Simkins. M., *The Roman Army from Hadrian to Constantine*, London (1979).

Simkins. M., *Warriors of Rome*, London (1988).

Smith R. E., *The Army Reforms of Septimius Severus*, Historia 21 (1972).

Somerset Fry. P., *Roman Britain*, Newton Abbot (1984).

Southern. P. and Dixon. K., *The Late Roman Army*, London (1996).

Southern. P., *The Numeri of the Roman Imperial Army*, Brit. 20 (1989).

Spaul. J. E. H., *ALA. The Auxiliary Cavalry Units of the Pre-Diocletianic Imperial Roman Army*, Andover (1994).

Speidel. M. A., *Roman Army Pay Scales*, J.R.S. 82 (1992).

Speidel. M. P., *Die Denkmäler der Kaiserreiter Equites Singulares Augusti*, Köln (1994).

Speidel. M. P., *Eagle Bearer and Trumpeter*, B. J. 176 (1976).

Speidel. M. P., *Horsemen in the Pannonian Alae*, Saalburg Jahrbuch 43 (1987)

Speidel. M. P., *The rise of Ethnic Units in the Roman Army*, A.N.R.W. II, 3, Berlin (1975).

Speidel. M. P. *Die Equites Singulares Augusti*, Bonn (1965).

Speidel. M. P., *Exploratores: Mobile elite units of Roman Germany*, in Roman Army Studies 2, Stuttgart (1992).

Speidel. M. P., *Nubias Roman Garrison*, A.N.R.W. II, 10, Berlin (1988).

Speidel. M. P., *Riding for Caesar. The Roman Emperors Horse Guard*, London (1994).

Speidel. M. P., *Roman Army Studies 1*, Amsterdam (1984).

Speidel. M. P., *Roman Army Studies 2*, Stuttgart (1992).

Speidel. M. P., *Swimming the Danube under Hadrians eyes*, Ancient Society 22 (1991).

Speidel. M. P., *The Pay of the Auxilia*, J.R.S. 63 (1973).

Speidel. M. P., *The Soldiers Servants*, Ancient Society 20 (1989).

Speidel. M. P., *The Weapons Keeper, the Fisci Curator and the ownership of weapons in the Roman Army*, in Roman Army Studies 2, Stuttgart (1992).

Starr. C., *The Roman Imperial Navy*, New York (1941).

Stoneman. R., *Palmyra and its Empire. Zenobia's Revolt against Rome*, Michigan (1992).

Strickland. T., *The Romans at Wilderspool*, Warrington (1995).

Strong. D. and Brown. D., *Roman Crafts*, London (1976).

Stuart. P., *Provincie Van een Imperium*, Leiden (1986).

Sulimirski. T., *The Sarmatians*, London (1970).

Sumner. G., *Roman Auxiliaries Reconstructed*, Military Illustrated 81 (1995).

Sumner. G., *The Roman Camel Corps*, Military Illustrated 90 (1995).

Tarradell. M., *Arte Romano en Espana*, Barcelona (1969).

Tomlin. R., *The later Roman Empire*, in *Warfare in the Ancient World*, Hackett. J. ed., London (1989).

Toynbee. J. M. C. *Animals in Roman Life and Art*, London (1973).

Toynbee. J. M. C. and Clarke. R. R., *A Roman decorated helmet and other objects from Norfolk*, J.R.S. 38 (1948).

Ulbert. G., *Gladii aus Pompeji*, Germania 47 (1969).

Ubl. H., *Was trug der Römische Soldat unter dem Cingulum*, in Van Driel-Murray. C. ed. (1989).

Ulbert. G., *Das römische Donau-Kastell Risstissen*, Stuttgart (1970).

Van Boekel. G., *Roman Terracotta horse figurines as a source for the Reconstruction of Harnessing*, in Van Driel-Murray. C. ed. (1989).

Van Driel-Murray. C., *A Fragmentary Shield Cover from Caerleon*, in Coulston. J. C. ed. (1988).

Van Driel-Murray. C. ed., *Roman Military Equipment: the Sources of Evidence.* Proceedings of the Fifth Roman Military Equipment Conference, B.A.R. Int. Ser. 476, Oxford (1989).

Van Driel-Murray. C. and Haas P. de., *A Circular Shield Cover and the Reconstruction of the accompanying Shield*, Exercitus 2.7 (1989).

Van Driel-Murray. C., *Leather Work in the Roman Army*, Exercitus 2 (1987).

Van Driel-Murray. C., *Shoes in Perspective*, S.M.R. (1986).

Van Driel-Murray. C., *The Roman Army Tent*, Exercitus 2.8 (1990).

Van Enckevort. H. and Willem W. J. H., *Roman Cavalry Helmets in Ritual Hoards from the Kops Plateau at Nijmegen, the Netherlands*, J.R.M.E.S. 5 (1994).

Vermeulle. C., *Hellenistic and Roman Cuirassed Statues*, Boston (1980).

Vogel. L., *The Column of Antoninus Pius*, Harvard (1973).

Waser. G., *Römische Inschrift-Kunst*, Stuttgart (1988).

Watson. G. R., *The Roman Soldier*, London (1969).

Waurick. G., *Soldaten in der Römischen Kunst*, in Hanson. W. S. and Keppie. L. eds. (1980).

Waurick. G., *Der Römische Helm in antike Helm*, Mainz (1988).

Webster. G., *A note on the Roman Cuirass*, Journal of the Arms and Armour Society 3 (1960).

Webster. G., *Decorated Dagger Scabbards found in Britain*, Exercitus 2.2. (1986).

Webster. G., *Standards and Standard Bearers in the Alae*, B. J. 186 (1986).

Webster. G., *The Roman Imperial Army*, London (1969).

Weinberg. S., *A hoard of Roman Armour*, Antike Kunst, (1979).

White. M., *Pompeii Scabbards (some reconstructions)*, Exercitus 3.2 (1996).

White. M., *The Fulham Sword*, Exercitus 2.9 (1992).

White. M., *The Usk Mail Hook reconstruction*, Exercitus 3.1 (1995).

White. M., *Reconstruction of Phalerae as a Military Award*, Exercitus 1.9. (1984).

Wilcox. P., *Rome's Enemies (2) Gallic and British Celts*, London (1985)

Wilcox. P., *Rome's Enemies, Germanics and Dacians*, London (1982).

Wilcox. P., *Rome's Enemies (3) Parthians and Sassanid Persians*, London (1986).

Wild. J. P., *A find of Roman Scale Armour from Carpow*, Brit. 12 (1981).

Wild. J. P., *Button and loop fasteners in the Roman Provinces*, Brit. 1 (1970).

Wild. J. P., *Clothing in the North-West Provinces of the Roman Empire*, B.J. 168 (1968).

Winterbottom. S., *Saddle Covers, Chamfrons and possible horse armour from Carlisle*, in Van Driel-Murray. C. ed. (1989).

Yadin. Y., *Bar-Kokba*, London (1971).

Yadin. Y., *Masada*, London (1966).

Zienkiewicz. D., *Roman Legion*, Cardiff (1994).

Roman Army Directory

Museums and Sites

All of the following are either devoted to the display of Roman Military equipment or contain items of related interest within their overall collection of contemporary material.

United Kingdom

The British Museum, Great Russell Street, London, WC1B 3DG. Telephone: 0171 636 1555.

The Roman Army Museum (Carvoran), Greenhead Via Carlisle, CA6 7JB. Telephone: 016972 485.

Grosvenor Museum, 27 Grosvenor Museum, Chester, CH1 2DD. Telephone: 01244 321616.

Corinium Museum, Park Street, Cirencester, Gloucestershire, GL7 2BX. Telephone: 01285 5611.

Colchester and Essex Museum, The Castle, Colchester, Essex, C01 1JJ. Telephone: 01206 576071.

Museum of Antiquities of The University and The Society of Antiquaries of Newcastle upon Tyne, The University, Newcastle upon Tyne, NE1 7RU. Telephone: 0191 222 6000.

The Lunt Roman Fort, Coventry Road, Bagington. For information contact The Herbert Art Gallery and Museum, Jordan Well, Coventry, CV1 5QP. Telephone: 01203 303507.

National Museum of Wales, Cathays Park, Cardiff, CF1 3NB. Telephone 01222 397951.

Roman Legionary Museum, High Street, Caerleon, Gwent, NP6 1AE. Telephone: 01633 423134.

Museum of London, London Wall, London EC2Y 5HN. Telephone: 0171 600 3699.

Royal Museum of Scotland, Queen Street, Edinburgh, EH2 1JD. Telephone: 0131 225 7534.

Yorkshire Museum, Museum Gardens, York, Y01 2DR. Telephone: 01904 29745.

Verulamium Museum, St Michael's, St Albans, Hertfordshire, AL3 4SW. Telephone: 01727 54659.

Right.

A reconstructed *Imaginifer* and *Signifer* showing a detail of the small round shield associated with both standard bearers and musicians.

Opposite.

Third century AD, infantry equipment reconstructed for the Archaeological Park at Carnuntum. The large oval shields are based on a number of examples from Dura Europos. Some infantry and cavalry units at this date appear to have worn very similar equipment.

Tullie House Museum, Castle Street, Carlisle, Telephone 01228 34787.

Senhouse Roman Museum, The Battery, Sea Brows, Maryport, Cumbria, CA15 6JD. Telephone: 01900 816168.

Housesteads Fort and Museum, Haydon Bridge, Hexham, Northumberland, NE47 6NN. For information contact Corbridge Roman Site Museum.

Manor House, Castle Yard, Ilkley, West Yorkshire, LS29 9DT. Telephone 01943 600066.

Corbridge Roman Site Museum, Corbridge, Northumberland, NE45 5NT. Telephone: 0143 441 3168.

Chesters Roman Fort and Museum, Chollerford, Hexham, Northumberland, NE46 4EP. For information contact Corbridge Roman Site Museum.

Vindolanda Fort and Museum, Chesterholm, Bardon Mill, Hexham, Northumberland, NE47 7JN. Telephone: 01454 344 277.

South Shields Roman Fort and Museum, Baring Street, South Shields, Tyne and Wear, NE33 2BB. Telephone 0191 454 4093.

Ribchester Museum, Riverside, Ribchester, Preston, Lancashire, PR3 3XS. Telephone 01254 878261.

Malton Museum, Market Place, Malton.

Segontium Roman Fort Museum, Beddgelert Road, Caernarfon. For information contact National Museum of Wales, Cardiff.

Doncaster Museum and Art Gallery, Chequer Road, Doncaster.

Rougemont House Museum, Castle Street, Exeter.

The Hunterian Museum, University of Glasgow, Glasgow G12 8QQ. Telephone: 0141 330 4221.

Richborough Roman Site, Sandwich, Kent, CT 13 9JW. For further information contact English Heritage, 1 High Street, Tonbridge, Kent, TN9 1SG.

At many English Heritage properties numerous large scale displays or mini events are organised throughout most of the year. Some of these events are educationally orientated and are relevant to historical topics within the National Curriculum. For details on events, specifically those which feature Roman Societies represented within this book, contact the Special Events Information line 0171 973 3396, or for general enquires on English Heritage contact English Heritage, 429 Oxford Street, London W1R 2HD. Telephone 0171 973 3434.

Austria

Archäologischer Park Carnuntum, Hauptstrasse 465, A-Pertonell-Carnuntum.

France

Musée des Antiquitiés Nationales, Château de Saint-Germain, 78103 Saint-Germain-en Layne, Yvelines.

Musée de la Civilisation Gallo-Romaine, 17 Rue Clæberg, 69005 Lyon.

Germany

Gauboden und Straubing Museum, Fraunhoferstrasse 9, 8440 Straubing.

Landesmuseum Mainz, Grosse Bleiche 49-51, 6500 Mainz.

Rheinisches Landesmuseum, Colmanstrasse 14-16, 5300 Bonn.

Limesmuseum, St Johannastrasse 5, 7080 Aalen.

Römisch-Germanisches Zentralmuseum, Kürfürstliches Schloss, Ernst Ludwig-Platz 2, 6500 Mainz.

Württembergisches Landesmuseum Stuttgart, Altes Schloss, 7000 Stuttgart.

Museum Burg Linn, Rheinbabenstrasse 85, 47809 Krefeld.

Kulturgeschichtliches Museum Osnabrück, Heger-Tor-Wall 28, 49078 Osnabrück.

Clemens-Sels-Museum, Am Obertor, 41460 Neuss.

Römisch-Germanisches Museum, Roncalliplatz 4, 50667 Köln.

Römer-und Pelizaeus-Museum, Am Steine 1-2, 31134 Hildesheim.

Saalburgmuseum, D-6380 Saalburg-Kastell.

Frühistorische Staatssammlung München. Lerchentekistr.2, D-80538 München.

Archäologischer Park Xanten, Am Amphitheater, 46509 Xanten.

Westfälisches Römermuseum Haltern, Weseler Strasse 100, 45721 Haltern.

Netherlands

Provinciaal Museum G.M. Kam, Museum Kamstraat 45 NL 6522 GB, Nijmegen.

Rijksmuseum Van Oudheden, Rapenburg 28, 2311 EW Leiden.

Switzerland

Vindonissa Museum, Museumstrasse 1. 5200 Brugg, Aaragau.

Bulgaria
Natsionalen Arheologitcheski Muzej BAN, bul. A1.
Stambolijski 2, 1000 Sofia.

Croatia
Arheoloski Muzej Zagret, Trg Nikole Zrinjskog 19,
41000 Zagreb.

Societies, Journals and Publications
Council for British Archaeology, Bowes Morrell
House, 111 Walmgate, York YO1 2UA. Publishes a
magazine *British Archaeology* ten times a year and *CBA
Briefing* five times a year, annual membership £18.00.

'*ALA* II *Flavia & LEGIOXXI RAPAX*'. Dr Marcus
Junkelmann. Schloss Ratzenhofen. 84094
Elsendorf. Germany.

Arbeia Society, Arbeia Roman fort and Museum, Baring
Street, South Shields, Tyne and Wear. NE33 2BB.
Telephone: 0191 454 4093. Publishes the *Arbeia*
magazine twice a year and the *Arbeia Journal*
annually. Subscription is £7.50. Membership of the
Society is £8.50 annually. Alternatively
membership of *Quinta* (Cohors V Gallorum) is
£9.50 annually. Membership of either society
includes all three publications.

Arma Newsletter of The Roman Military Equipment
Conference. Available from M. C. Bishop,
Braemar, Kirkgate, Chirnside, Duns, TD11 3XL.
Telephone 01890 818197. Published twice yearly.
Subscription £5.00.

Journal of Roman Military Equipment Studies, Published
annually, available from Oxbow Books, Park End
Place, Oxford OX1 1HN. Stockists of new and
second hand archaeological publications.

Society for The Promotion of Roman Studies, Institute of
Archaeology, 31/34 Gordon Square, London,
WC1H OPY. Telephone: 0171 387 8157.
Publishes two yearly publications.
The Journal of Roman Studies: covering many
aspects of Roman history including the military.
Subscription £25.00.
Britannia: Dealing with the latest excavations in
Great Britain, includes military finds as discovered.
Subscription £25.00 or £40.00 for both journals.

The Ermine Street Guard, award winning re-enactment
group founded in 1972. Contact address: Chris
Haines, Oakland Farm, Dog Lane, Witcombe,
Gloucestershire, GL3 4UG. Telephone: 01452
862235. Membership £10.00 per year, publishes
Exercitus which features articles on practical
research into the Roman army.

The Gemina Project, Kaiserstraat 8G, 2311GR Leiden,
The Netherlands.

Roman Army Research Group of London, 7 Coalecroft
Road, London, SW15 6LW.

Legio IX *Hispana*, 3210 32nd St, San Diego, California,
92104-4736 USA.

Twentieth Legion, 9416 Rhode Island Ave, College
Park, MD 20740-1639 USA.

Legio XIIII *Gemina Martia Victrix*, Freiherr Von Stien
Str, 22, 55774 Baumholder, Germany.

The Internet

on the World Wide Web

Armamentarium
The book of Roman Arms and Armour
http://ww.ncl.ac.Uk/~nantig/arma

Romansites-L
Romansites-L lists all Roman Web sites, send email to
Petworth @ suba.com and the message SUBSCRIBE
Romansites-L including your name.

ArmaList
Send email to *armamentarium @ poboxes.com* with the
subject of ArmaList in the body of the message put
subscribe ArmaList your name @ your place.
Further details are also available on the *ArmaList
home page.*

Romarch
send email to *majordomo @rome.classics.lsa.umich.edu*
with the message subscribe Romarch.
Internet Archaeology, Department of Archaeology,
University of York, The Kings Manor, York YO1
2EP.
email: *editor @ intarch.ac.UK.*

Index

Acknowledgements

The author would like to thank 'The Ermine Street
Guard' in particular Chris Haines and Martin White
for their helpful advice and encouragement. The
members of 'Quinta' and Dr Marcus Junkelmann for
generous use of his photographs without which the
section on Sports equipment would have been
decidedly bare. I am also grateful to Mike Bishop and
Simon James for their useful suggestions and
supplying information and to the artist Graham
Turner for his evocative paintings. I should like to
thank the following for allowing me to use
photographs from their collections; The Board of
Trustees of the National Museums and Galleries on
Merseyside (Walker Art Gallery); The British Film
Institute; P.C. Film Corp New York; The British
Museum; Chester City Council, Grosvenor Museum;
Geoff Wills, Paul Karremans of the Gemina Project.
Special thanks must go to Paul Holder of the John
Rylands University Library, Manchester who
answered many requests for sources of information
and found many obscure references and who along
with Mike Bishop also found time to proof read the
text. Nearly all of their suggestions have been
incorporated into this work. All of the line drawings
and remaining Photographs are by the author. Finally
I would like to thank Denise Rowntree who was able
to translate my scrawl at short notice and type this
manuscript, the editor Tim Newark, Brasseys (UK)
and most of all Elaine for her patience.